Foundations of the Faith

The Rt. Rev. William C. Wantland

Morehouse-Barlow Co., Inc.
Wilton, Connecticut 06897

Copyright © 1983 William C. Wantland

All rights reserved. No part of this publication
may be reproduced, stored in a retrieval system,
or transmitted in any form or by any means, electronic,
mechanical, photocopying, recording, or otherwise,
without the prior permission of the copyright owner.

Morehouse-Barlow Co., Inc.
78 Danbury Road
Wilton, Connecticut 06897

ISBN 0-8192-1320-9
Library of Congress Catalog Card Number 82-61889
Printed in the United States of America

Table of Contents

Introduction	5
Part I Holy Scripture	**11**
Chapter 1 The Bible	13
Part II The Creeds	**33**
Chapter 2 The Holy Trinity, the Incarnation and the Church	35
Chapter 3 Scriptural Basis for the Creeds	59
Part III The Sacraments	**71**
Chapter 4 Christian Initiation	75
Chapter 5 The Eucharist	99
Chapter 6 Other Sacramental Rites	123
Part IV The Ministry	**131**
Chapter 7 The Threefold Ministry of Apostolic Succession	133
Afterword	165
Appendix: "Dialogues" and Foundations of the Faith	167
Bibliography	185

INTRODUCTION

Christians have long been concerned about the divisions which exist in the body of Christ. Our divided status is felt by many to be in direct conflict with the wish of Our Lord when He prayed, "That they all may be one."

The Anglican Communion has been in the forefront of the search for Christian unity. True unity has been a real concern for Anglicans. However, Anglicans see a sacramental sharing and spiritual life together as growing from an already existing theological unity. This view is focused in Resolution 42 of the worldwide Lambeth Conference of the Anglican Bishops meeting in 1930, which held "as a general principle that the intercommunion should be the goal of, rather than a means to, the restoration of union." This was reaffirmed in the declaration of the 1968 Lambeth Conference of Anglican Bishops: "Reciprocal intercommunion (is) allowable... (only) where there is agreement on apostolic faith and order." If, then, we are to strive for Christian unity as the prayer of Our Lord, and if that unity requires agreement on apostolic faith and order, is there any basis by which Anglicans can measure that essential bedrock of belief?

In 1961, the General Convention of the Episcopal Church declared that persons selected to represent the Church in dialogue with other Christian bodies:

> "be reminded of the various historic statements defining this Church's stand in the field of Christian reunion beginning with the Chicago version of the Quadrilateral in 1886 and including several statements by successive Lambeth Conferences, particularly the Faith and Order Statement prepared by the Commission itself for the Lambeth Conference "of 1948 and the General Conven-

tion of 1949; and ... be ... instructed to make the historic position of this Church as defined in these several statements the framework for all Church unity conversations in which it shall be engaged."

This position was reaffirmed by the National Consultation on Ecumenism in the Local Church, meeting in November of 1981.

For Episcopalians, then, the basis of our faith is to be found in the Chicago Quadrilateral adopted by the House of Bishops meeting at Chicago 1886, and as expanded by subsequent actions of Lambeth Conference and our own General Convention. (A quadrilateral is a four-sided geometric figure. The "Chicago Quadrilateral" therefore means the four sides or points of the Christian Faith essential to unity as defined by the House of Bishops in Chicago.)

All Episcopalians who seek after Christian unity are called to know the provisions of this Quadrilateral; further, all other Christians should also be familiar with it, as it contains the Anglican understanding of the apostolic faith and order which is a prerequisite for any real Christian unity. It is the purpose of this book to acquaint Christians, Anglican and non-Anglican alike, with the essentials or foundations of the Christian Faith as defined in the Chicago-Lambeth Quadrilateral. Let us therefore look at the 1886 Chicago Statement:

"We, Bishops of the Protestant Episcopal Church in the United States of America, in Council assembled as Bishops in the Church of God, do hereby solemnly declare to all whom it may concern, and especially to our fellow-Christians of the different Communions in the land, who, in their several spheres, have contended for the religion of Christ:

1. Our earnest desire that the Saviour's prayer, 'That we all may be one,' may, in its deepest and truest sense, be speedily fulfilled;

2. That we believe that all who have been duly baptized with water, in the name of the Father, and of the Son, and of the Holy Ghost, are members of the Holy Catholic Church;

3. That in all things of human ordering or human choice, relating to modes of worship and discipline, or to tradi-

tional customs, this Church is ready in the spirit of love and humility to forgo all preferences of her own;

4. That this Church does not seek to absorb other Communions, but rather co-operating with them on the basis of a common Faith and Order, to discountenance schism, to heal the wounds of the Body of Christ, and to promote the charity which is the chief of Christian graces and the visible manifestation of Christ to the world;

But furthermore, we do hereby affirm that the Christian unity . . . can be restored only by the return of all Christian communions to the principles of unity exemplified by the undivided Catholic Church during the first ages of its existence; which principles we believe to be the substantial deposit of Christian Faith and Order committed by Christ and his Apostles to the Church unto the end of the world, and therefore incapable of compromise or surrender by those who have been ordained to be its stewards and trustees for the common and equal benefit of all men.

As inherent parts of this sacred deposit, and therefore as essential to the restoration of unity among the divided branches of Christendom, we account the following, to wit: (These are the four sides, or points, of the Quadrilateral.)

1. The Holy Scriptures of the Old and New Testament as the revealed Word of God.

2. The Nicene Creed as the sufficient statement of the Christian Faith.

3. The two Sacraments—Baptism and the Supper of the Lord—ministered with unfailing use of Christ's words of institution and of the elements ordained by Him.

4. The Historic Episcopate, locally adapted in the methods of its administration to the varying needs of the nations and peoples called of God into the unity of His Church.

Furthermore, deeply grieved by the sad divisions which affect the Christian Church in our own land, we hereby declare our desire and readiness, so soon as there shall be any authorized response to this Declaration, to enter into brotherly conference with all or any Christian Bodies seeking the restoration of the organic unity of the Church, with a view to the earnest study of the conditions under which so priceless a blessing might happily be brought to pass."

This statement, made by the Episcopal Bishops in Chicago, became the basis of the Lambeth Declaration, in Resolution No. 11, adopted by Lambeth Conference in 1888. From that day it has been called the Lambeth or Chicago-Lambeth Quadrilateral. The Anglican Communion, then, has committed itself to a quest for union based upon what we now call the Chicago-Lambeth Quadrilateral.

A restatement of the Quadrilateral by Lambeth Conference in 1920 led directly to the Lausanne Conference of 1927 and the development of the Faith and Order Movement.

In 1930, Lambeth Conference further defined the historic episcopate as "the episcopate as it emerged in the clear light of history from the time when definite evidence begins to be available ... The historic episcopate as we understand it goes behind the perversions of history to the original conceptions of the Apostolic ministry."

In 1948, the Episcopal Joint Commission on Approaches to Unity was directed to reformulate the basis of unity on which the Episcopal Church would be prepared to negotiate with other Churches, and did so in a report to the 1948 Lambeth Conference and General Convention of 1949. The reformulation went back to the four points of the Quadrilateral, expanding each of them. In regard to the third point on the Sacraments, the Commission added that "the Church recognizes sacramental rites or mysteries, namely, confirmation, absolution, the marriage blessing, Holy Orders, and the unction of the sick." The historic episcopate was further defined, and to it were added sections on the Priesthood and Diaconate.

The current thinking of the Episcopal Church on the Chicago-Lambeth Quadrilateral is set forth in the "Detroit Report," the statement of the National Ecumenical Consultation of the Episcopal Church, meeting in November of 1978. Refined for presentation to the 1979 General Convention, the Resolution drawn from the Report was further amended and referred to the Inter-Anglican Theological and Doctrinal Advisory. It is now being studied by the several autonomous Provinces of the Anglican Communion, and was approved by the General Convention of the Episcopal Church in September of 1982.

After re-affirming the Chicago-Lambeth Quadrilateral as printed on pages 876-878 of the Prayer Book "as a statement of essential principles for organic unity with other churches," General Convention affirmed "the following as an explication of that basic document without denying anything contained therein":

"1. The Holy Scriptures of the Old and New Testament are . . . the authoritative norm for catholic faith in Jesus Christ and for the doctrinal tradition of the Gospel. Therefore, we declare that they contain all things necessary for salvation.

"2. The Apostles' and Nicene Creeds are the form through which the Christian Church . . . under the guidance of the Holy Spirit, understood, interpreted, and expressed its faith in the Triune God. The continuing doctrinal tradition is . . . to understand, interpret and express its faith in continuity and consistency with these ancient creeds . . .

"3. The Church is the sacrament of God's presence in the world. . . . That presence . . . (is) made active and real in the Church . . . through the Gospel sacraments of Baptism and Eucharist, as well as other sacramental rites . . .

"4. . . . Apostolic *ministry* exists to promote, safeguard, and serve apostolic teaching . . . In order to serve, lead, and enable this ministry, some are set apart and ordained in the historic orders of Bishop, Presbyter, and Deacon. We understand the historic episcopate as central to this apostolic ministry and essential to the reunion of the Church . . . Bishops in apostolic succession are, therefore, the focus and personal symbols of this inheritance . . ."

Thus, the Episcopal Church has set forth and maintained certain principles as "the substantial deposit of Christian Faith and Order" which are "incapable of compromise or surrender," principles which are "essential to the restoration of unity," "exemplified by the undivided Catholic Church during the first ages of its existence."

Those essentials may be restated as follows:

1. Holy Scripture as "containing all things necessary for salvation."

2. The Apostles' and Nicene Creeds, as effectual statements of the Catholic Faith.

3. The two Sacraments of Our Lord, Baptism and the Holy Eucharist, together with those five "commonly called Sacraments," namely Confirmation, Holy Matrimony, Penance, Holy Orders and Unction.

4. The threefold ministry of Apostolic Succession, consisting of Bishops, Priests and Deacons.

In the chapters that follow we shall examine the Christian Faith in the light of these four essentials of the Church. We can only seek a true and lasting unity of Christendom if we first understand the essentials of the Faith, and realize that any plan of union must be based on those essentials. Any so-called "unity" which is not based on a mutual understanding of the Christian Religion is no real unity. Only if we agree on what Christianity really is, can we "all be one." Only if we know what we truly believe, can we hope to agree. Let us therefore study the foundations of our Faith: Scriptures, Creeds, Sacraments and Ministry.

PART I

Holy Scriptures

Article VI of the Articles of Religion states:

"Holy Scripture containeth all things necessary to salvation: so that whatsoever is not read therein, nor may be proved thereby, is not to be required of any man, that it should be believed as an article of the Faith, or be thought requisite or necessary to salvation. In the name of the Holy Scripture we do understand those canonical Books of the Old and New Testament, of whose authority was never any doubt in the Church . . .

"And the other Books (as Hierome saith) the Church doth read for example of life and instruction of manners; but yet doth it not apply them to establish any doctrine . . .

"All the Books of the New Testament, as they are commonly received, we do receive, and account them Canonical."

In the following chapter, we will examine the history, structure and authority of the Bible in the life of the Church. However, our review of Scripture will not be limited to this section; Scriptures will be cited throughout this work as basic authority for the teaching of the Church. It is the purpose of chapter 1 only to outline the role of the Bible as one of the essential deposits of the Faith.

CHAPTER 1

The Bible

We began the introduction to this section by quoting Article VI of the Articles of Religion concerning the authority and role of Holy Scripture in the life of the Church. In order to understand the statement of Article VI, it will be necessary to look at the actual history of the development of Holy Scripture. How did we get the Bible?

First, the word "Bible" comes from a Greek word, *Biblia*, which is the plural for the Greek word meaning "book." *Biblia* therefore means "library" or "collection of books." This is precisely what the Bible is, a collection of books.

Secondly, the collection is arranged in a list or "canon" (the word "canon" comes from a Greek word meaning "list"). Books officially included on the list are therefore "canonical" as the Article states.

Thirdly, the word "Bible" implies much more than just a canon or list of books. The Bible, as a unit, is seen as a special collection of *inspired* writings, the Holy Word. The Bible is therefore an agreed collection of those writings that are seen to be the inspired Word of God. This does not mean that as soon as a Book of the Bible was written that people immediately declared, "This is the Holy Word." To the contrary, it took literally centuries for different writings to become accepted as part of Holy Scripture.

The Old Testament has historically been divided into three parts: the Law *(Torah)*, the Prophets *(Nebi 'im)* and the writings *(Kethubim)*. Of these parts, the first written was the Law. However, even the Law was not written until many centuries after the beginning of God's revelation of himself to the Hebrew people.

Tradition and historical theory trace the Aramean ancestors of Israel to the district of Ur, on the lower Euphrates River.

About 2350 B.C., a group of these tribes emigrated to the area now know as Haran, Turkey. ("Terah took his son Abram . . . and they set out from Ur . . . for the land of Canaan. But when they reached Harran, they settled there" Gen. xi. 31.) Some of the tribes, traditionally belonging to the Joseph group, wandered to the borders of Egypt, during the period of the invader Hyksos kings, between 1700 and 1600 B.C. It is during this period that Joseph apparently went into Egypt. Joseph became a great leader in Egypt, so great that the Pharaoh made him the second most powerful man in the kingdom (Gen. xli. 40). Genesis tells quite clearly the story of Joseph being joined in Egypt by his Hebrew family. However, after the death of Joseph, and around 1580 B.C., the Hyksos were defeated and expelled under Ahmose I. The new Theban ruler and his followers had nothing to do with their former overlords, and were not kindly disposed to the Arameans within their midst. This explains the comment in the Book of Exodus, "Then a new king ascended the throne of Egypt, one who knew nothing of Joseph" (Ex. i. 8).

For the next three hundred years the Hebrews were in captivity, until they were led out of Egypt during the reign of Ramses II by Moses. The date given is around 1290 to 1280 B.C. Apparently the Hebrews were a number of years finally reaching Canaan, the original goal of Abraham. Exodus tells us they were some 40 years in the wilderness, and historical evidence indicates movement into Canaan around 1250 to 1240 B.C. The Hebrews continued their conquest and settlement of Palestine from 1250 to around 1200 B.C. with the rise of the Judges. Israel was ruled by the Judges until 1020 B.C., when Saul was crowned the first king. Israel remained a united kingdom until the death of Solomon in 922 B.C. This occasioned the division of the kingdom into two states, Judah and Israel.

Israel (the northern kingdom) was finally destroyed by the Assyrians in the eighth century B.C. The last hold out was Samaria, which fell in 721 B.C. The defeated Israelites were taken into captivity to become the "lost tribes." The remnants of people intermarried with Mesopotamian immigrants and became the Samaritans, a mixed-blood people holding to the basic tenets of the Israelite religion.

Only the southern kingdom of Judah remained, and it was to be utterly destroyed under Nebuchadnezzar in 586 B.C.

This is the famous "Babylonian Captivity," which is considered to have lasted until the rebuilding of the Temple of Solomon in Jerusalem in 516 B.C.

Finally, in 444 B.C., Nehemiah returns to Jerusalem as Governor, and during the same period, Ezra came to Jerusalem from Babylon. He was "a scribe learned in the law of Moses" who had come "entrusted with the law of God" (Ezra vii. 6, 14). This law was the *Torah*, or first five Books of our present Old Testament.

These five Books, called the Pentateuch, were the result of great oral tradition going back to the origins of the Creation story, the Flood, Abraham and the unwritten history which followed. The oral tradition was written down gradually, and Biblical scholars have discovered at least four different source documents for the Pentateuch. These documents are referred to as J, E, D and P.

The oldest of these documents, J, is so called because it commonly uses the name Yahweh for God (transliterated as Jehovah, hence "J"). It dates from about 850 B.C. The next document is called E from the use of Elohim for the word God. It was written around 750 B.C. The next, D, is so called from the name of the Book discovered in 621 B.C. by King Josiah, namely Deuteronomy. The last document is P so called because it is a Priestly one. Thus, the Pentateuch (Five Books), also known as the Torah, or Law, had been written over a period from 850 B.C. to 440 B.C. However, the oral history for the written word goes back many centuries earlier, as can be seen from our thumb-nail sketch of Jewish history. It is this unwritten tradition which, when finally put in written form and edited (largely during the Babylonian Captivity), becomes the "Law" brought to Jerusalem by Ezra.

These five Books (Genesis, Exodus, Leviticus, Numbers and Deuteronomy) were the first Scripture of the Jews. Indeed, this was the primary sum of the Bible at the end of the fifth century B.C. For example, by 400 B.C, the Samaritans and the Jews had separated: at this point, the two groups shared a common Bible. The Samaritan Scripture still consists solely of the Pentateuch.

The second part of the Hebrew Bible is *Nebi'im*, the Prophets. This part is further divided into what is called the "Former Prophets" and the "Latter Prophets."

The Former Prophets consist of the Books of Joshua, Judges,

First and Second Samuel, and First and Second Kings. While these Books would be seen by us as more historical than prophetic, they do include stories of great prophets such as Samuel, Nathan, Elijah and Elisha. The Latter Prophets include Isaiah, Jeremiah, Ezekiel, and the "twelve minor prophets," Hosea, Joel, Amos, Obadiah, Jonah, Micah, Nahum, Habakkuk, Zephaniah, Haggai, Zechariah and Malachi. They are referred to as minor prophets, not because they are less important than the others, but because of the shortness of the Books; minor here means short.

These books began to be written down around the eighth century B.C., and a number of them would have been in existence when Ezra returned to Jerusalem. Indeed, surviving Samaritan literature indicates that they knew of the existence of the former Prophets. However, they were not part of the canon of Scripture at the time of the Samaritan schism.

The earliest references to the Prophets as a definite collection are found shortly after 200 B.C. In Ecclesiasticus, written around 180 B.C., the "twelve prophets" are referred to as parallel to Jeremiah and Ezekial (Ecclus. xlix. 10). Jeremiah is cited in Daniel (Dan. ix. 2) as authoritative. The Book of Daniel was written around 168 B.C. It would therefore be safe to state that the Prophets became accepted as canonical around 200 B.C.

The third division of the Old Testament is that collection of Books we call the Writings *(Kethubim)*. Ecclesiasticus, cited above, was written by Jesus Ben Sirach. Later in the second century (132 B.C.), Ben Sirach's grandson translated Ecclesiasticus into the Greek language. In the preface he mentioned that his grandfather studied "the law, the prophets, and the other writings of our ancestors." It is thus held that by the second century, the Old Testament was already divided into the three parts we have mentioned.

The writings include Psalms, Proverbs, Job, Ecclesiastes, the Song of Solomon, Ruth, Lamentations, Esther, Ezra, Nehemiah, First and Second Chronicles and Daniel. However, the reference to "other writings" indicated that this section of the Old Testament was not as yet clearly defined. While books such as Daniel and Psalms were admitted, books written later than 100 B.C., such as the so-called Psalms of Solomon (c. 50 B.C.) were denied admission. From this we can say that the (Palestinian) canon of writings was closed around 100 B.C.

This reference to the Palestinian canon requires further discussion. In addition to the Jewish peoples of Palestine, Jews were scattered throughout the known world. This situation goes back to at least the fourth century B.C. During the fourth century, Macedonia became the dominant world power. Alexander the Great, King of Macedonia, conquered virtually the whole known world. It was during this period that Persia fell to the Macedonians (331 B.C.). Judah (now the Province of Judea) became a province of the Greek empire. Alexander showed special consideration to the Jews. After the founding of Alexandria in Egypt, thousands of Jews migrated to this Egyptian city, creating a great Israelite colony. From here, the Jews, who had been given Greek citizenship, traveled to all the areas of the ancient world, establishing commercial colonies in every major trading city. In fact, so numerous were these migrations, that they became known collectively as the *Diaspora*, from the Greek word for "Dispersion."

These Jews had to learn the trade language of Greek, and lived in the Greek speaking parts of the world. It was in the next century that translations of the Hebrew Scripture began to be made into the Greek language. Indeed, this appeared necessary, as the Jews of the Dispersion had begun to use Greek even in their corporate worship. The translation of Scripture in the Greek is referred to as the Septuagint (Latin for Seventy) from the story that seventy scholars made the translation at Alexandria by order of Ptolemy II Philadelphus of Egypt. True or not, by the end of the second century B.C., the Old Testament existed in a Greek version, as well as the Hebrew one.

The Greek Old Testament included books not in the Hebrew one. Further, the organization of the Greek Bible was on somewhat different lines from the Hebrew Testament. The Septuagint was arranged, not in the three groups representing the stages of canonization, but according to subject matter. This arrangement was Law, History, Poetry and Prophecy. Within this arrangement, "other writings" were included, such as Tobit, Judith, First and Second Maccabees, three additions to Daniel, the Wisdom of Solomon, Ecclesiasticus, Baruch, First and Second Esdras (sometimes called Third and Fourth Esdras). This Greek Old Testament was known as the Alexandrian canon, as opposed to the Palestinian canon. It was the Alexandrian canon which Our Lord and the Apostles quoted in the New Testament.

For the Christian Church, then, there was a real question of what made up the sacred Scripture. The Church had both the larger (Alexandrian) canon and the smaller (Palestinian) canon. As the Christians generally preferred the Septuagint, or Greek larger canon (the New Testament was written in Greek), the Jewish Church tended to prefer the smaller Hebrew canon. For Judaism, the question was settled at the Council of Jamnia, an assembly of learned Rabbis meeting at the town of Jamnia in 90 A.D. At this Council, the Rabbis limited the Jewish Scripture to the books in the Palestinian Hebrew canon. The method of counting books was quite different from our present method. While our present Bible contains a thirty-nine-book Old Testament, the Jews counted these books as twenty-four. Thus:

Five Books of the Law.
Four Books of the Former Prophets (First and Second Samuel and First and Second Kings each considered one Book).
Four Books of the Latter Prophets (Twelve Minor Prophets being one Book).
Eleven Books of the Writings (Ezra and Nehemiah and First and Second Chronicles each considered one Book).

The idea of twenty-four Books continued right down to the writing of Article VI of the Articles of Religion. However, there has been some change. First and Second Samuel, First and Second Kings, and First and Second Chronicles are each treated as separate books. Ezra-Nehemiah is listed as two Books (First and Second Esdras). Five books (Isaiah, Daniel, Ezekiel, Jeremiah and Lamentations, attributed to Jeremiah, although actually part of the Writings, not Prophets), of the four "Greater Prophets, are lumped together and the Twelve "Lesser" Prophets are likewise lumped together as a single book. In any event, what we now count as the Old Testament was fully accepted by both Jews and Christians.

But what about the Apocrypha? What is its status in the Church? And how did it reach that status?

We saw earlier how the Jewish Church dealt with the matter. When faced with a choice between the more expanded

Alexandrian canon and the more restrictive Palestinian one, the Jews chose the restricted Hebrew canon. Doubtless, the choice was partly influenced by the fact that Jerusalem had been destroyed some twenty years earlier, and nationalistic interests would have opted for a strictly Hebrew Scripture. Futher, the Greek canon was being used by Christians, who were now totally excluded from the synagogues.

For the Christian, the matter was not so easy. While the Greek Testament was quoted by Our Lord and the Apostles, there is no known quotation from that portion of the Septuagint which we now call the Apocrypha. Further, though we have spoken of the Alexandrian canon, there was no final agreement as to all the books to be included. In one sense, the Alexandrian "canon" was not really a canon, or closed list of accepted Books.

Since the New Testament was written in Greek, the first Christian Bible used the Septuagint for the Old Testament. However, it was recognized by the early Church Fathers that there was a more limited Hebrew Old Testament. St. Jerome (refered to in Article VI) translated the Bible from Greek into Latin. In his work, Jerome listed those Books of the Hebrew canon, then stated: "Whatever is not included in this list is to be classed as apocryphal. Therefore Wisdom, commonly entitled of Solomon, the Book of Jesus the Son of Sirach, Judith and Tobit .. are not in the canon" (A.D. 384). However, the apocryphal books of the (Greek) Old Testament were translated into Latin and included in the Vulgate Bible of Jerome.

From this date forward, the place of the Apocrypha has been a matter of constant dispute. St. Augustine, for example, in his work *On Christian Doctrine*, includes as part of the Old Testament the Books of Judith, Tobit, First and Second Maccabees, Ecclesiasticus and Wisdom. While agreeing with Jerome that they were not in the Hebrew, nonetheless, he felt that they were truly Scripture.

Origen had taken much the same position. In his dispute with Julius Africanus, around 240 A.D., while admitting that the Story of Susanna was not in the Hebrew, and was not canonical in the same sense as Hebrew Scripture, he nevertheless argued that the Christian Church had always accepted these (Greek) books as edifying. This was finally the position of Jerome, as quoted in Article VI; i.e. these are books which the Church reads "for edification of the people, but not for the proving of the doctrines of the Church."

The Eastern Church had accepted the apocryphal Books as fully canonical until about the fourth century. At that time, however, the Eastern Fathers such as Eusebius, Athanasius, Cyril of Jerusalem and Gregory of Nazianzus, came to recognize a distinction between those of the Hebrew canon and the rest. For some centuries thereafter, the Eastern Church continued to give wide acceptance to the Apocrypha; but at the Synod of Jerusalem in 1672, only Tobit, Judith, Ecclesiasticus and Wisdom were held to be canonical.

In the Western Church, the distinction raised by Jerome was officially recognized, although most people ignored the distinction. As a result, the Council of Trent, in 1548, held that for Roman Catholics, all of the Apocrypha except Second Esdras and the Prayer of Manasses was to be counted canonical. On the other hand, the Church of England followed Jerome (as we saw in Article VI, above) in holding the Apocrypha is to be read "for example of life and instruction of manners; but . . . not . . . to establish any doctrine." While Luther's Bible, and some other early Protestant editions continued to print the Apocrypha, the Apocrypha came to be rejected completely by the Protestant Church. In 1643, the Westminster Confession entirely rejected the claim of the Apocrypha to be in any sense a part of Scripture. In 1827, the Presbyterian Church induced the British and Foreign Bible Society to adopt the policy of refusing to publish the Apocrypha.

The end result is a lack of final judgment by the whole Christian Church, even today. Roman Catholics utterly reject some of the Books of the Apocrypha and accept as totally canonical the rest; the Orthodox Church likewise, but with different books; the Protestant Church simply rejects the Apocrypha *in toto;* the Anglicans persist in following the ancient rule of Jerome in refusing canonical status to the Apocrypha, but continuing the use of *all* of the Apocrypha for edification. Old Catholics and some Lutherans follow the Anglican position.

However, there is a growing appreciation of the Apocrypha by the whole Christian Church. *The Oxford Dictionary of the Christian Church* says this of the Apocrypha:

> "With the growth of a historical perspective in Biblical studies in the 19th cent., . . . the great value of the Apocrypha as historical sources came to be generally

recognized, and there came also a new recognition of their religious value ... and as having been read as Scripture by the pre-Nicene Church and many post-Nicene Fathers, they have gained increasing respect even from those who do not hold them to be equally canonical with the rest of the (Old Testament)."

Also, we quote from Dr. William Barclay, outstanding Protestant Biblical scholar, in his book, *Introducing the Bible:*

"The Apocrypha have a place in the moral literature of the world .... The Apocrypha contain indispensable historical material, as for instance, the story of the struggle of the Maccabees for the freedom of the Jews. But the supreme use of the Apocrypha is that they bridge the gap between the Old and New Testaments. In that gap there are three hundred years of which we will know very little .... The great use of the Apocrypha is that they give us the political, cultural, ethical and religious background of the contemporaries of Jesus Christ, and therefore help us better to understand the New Testament.

"The importance of the Apocrypha cannot be doubted and no student of the Bible can afford to disregard them."

We now come to the formation of the New Testament. In many ways, we can draw a parallel with the development of the Old Testament.

The New Testament is traditionally divided into four major parts. First come the Gospels, then the Acts of the Apostles, the Epistles, and finally the Revelation of John. Unlike the Old Testament, this division does not reflect the order of canonization. Rather, it is a topical division, similar to the Alexandrian canon. As the Old Testament had an oral tradition which preceded the actual written Scripture, so also with the New. And as the Old Testament only gradually came to be gathered into a coherent, accepted whole, so also with the New.

Jesus of Nazareth was born at Bethlehem around 6-4 B.C., and was crucified in A.D. 29. Christian ministry began to spread the gospel (good news) of Christ immediately. Saul of Tarsus, former enemy of Christianity, was converted shortly after the martyrdom of Stephen the Deacon in A.D. 35. The great missionary journeys of Saul (now Paul) began around

A.D. 44. The first Church Council, the Council of Jerusalem, met in A.D. 49. At this time, not one word of New Testament Scripture had been written.

The earliest written section of the New Testament is that included under the title of "Epistles." While dating of New Testament Books is very problematic, the first Epistle written is generally felt to be St. Paul's Epistle to the Galatians, probably written around A.D. 49. (Some authorities would place this work later, around 58.) The next works are First and Second Thessalonians, written about eight months apart, in A.D. 51. There is no serious question about the authorship of these letters. Paul clearly wrote them. Other letters generally felt to be written by St. Paul include Romans, written c. 55; First Corinthians, written c. 54-55; Second Corinthians, written c. 55-56; Ephesians, probably written in Rome around A.D. 60; Colossians and Philemon, written in A.D. 60, also from Rome; and Philipians, written in A.D. 61.

As to the so-called Pastoral Epistles, First and Second Timothy and Titus, Pauline authorship is very much questioned. If he did write them, they would have to be dated prior to 65, the year of his martyrdom.

The Epistle to the Hebrews was never ascribed to St. Paul prior to the fourth century. The letter, itself, makes no such claim. It was apparently written by an Alexandrian Jew, possibly Apollos, somewhere between 60 and 70.

The Epistle General of St. James was written prior to 62 by James "the Lord's brother," not to be confused with James the Less, the Apostle.

First Peter is generally ascribed to the Prince of the Apostles, and dated around A.D. 64, shortly before his martyrdom.

The Epistle General of St. Jude was written by Judas, the "brother of James," and hence probably one of the "brethren of the Lord" (Mk. vi. 3). This Judas, or Jude, is not to be confused with Judas, Son of James, also called Thaddeus, one of the Twelve. No definite date can be ascribed to this work. However, the internal evidence would indicate a possible early date.

As to the remaining Epistles, First John was written by a person named John, and was generally held by the early Church to have been written by the Apostle, the "beloved Disciple." The date of the Epistle is unclear, but probably was written between 90 and 110.

With the three remaining Epistles, Second Peter was clearly

not written by Peter, but by someone under his name. The early Church largely rejected it, and it dates from the second century, probably between 125 and 150. Second and Third John were written by a person called John the Presbyter. The early Church was almost unanimous in stating that this John was not the same as the author of First John, the Gospel or Revelation. No positive date can be given, but the works are clearly second century.

Most of the Epistles were written between A.D. 49-50 and 65. Only one written after that date, First John, appears to be written by the author to whom it was ascribed.

The second section of the New Testament to be written is what we refer to as the Gospels. The earliest Gospel is that of St. Mark. Most authorities agree that John Mark wrote this Gospel, and that it was written shortly after 65. Apparently, Mark had been secretary to Peter, had heard Peter preach on numerous occasions, and decided to write what he had heard in order to preserve apostolic testimony when Peter was martyred in 65.

The next Gospel written is that "according to St. Matthew." Probably written sometime between 70 and 80, the work appears to be an editing of several sources, including Mark's Gospel. There is ancient evidence to believe that, in addition to Mark, the edited material included writings of Matthew which recorded the discourses and teachings of Jesus. Hence, the Gospel is ascribed to Matthew, although he almost certainly was not the author of the final document.

Luke's Gospel was written by Luke the "beloved physician" in the latter part of the first century, possibly around 80. This work was actually the first volume of a two volume treatise on the Christian Church. Volume two is commonly called the Acts of the Apostles, and was also written by St. Luke, shortly after the completion of his Gospel. There is no reason to doubt the authorship of either book.

The last Gospel is that of John. Probably written around 95, there is some internal evidence to believe that the largest part of the Gospel was written by John the Apostle, with other material added, possibly after John's death.

The third section of the New Testament, Acts, we have already mentioned. While it is classed separately from the Gospels, it really is a unity with the Gospel of Luke. The two were written as a unit, and should be read as a unit.

The last division of the New Testament is the Revelation of

John. This work was probably written around 95, by a person named John, However, scholars are still sharply divided as to whether the author is the Apostle, John the Presbyter (author of Second and Third John), or someone else. This confusion is nothing new, as the early Church was equally divided on the point.

Now that we have briefly reviewed the writing of the twenty-seven Books of the New Testament, we should look at the development of the New Testament list of Books, or canon. The earliest mention of anything like a canon is found in the writings of the heretic Marcion, around A.D. 140. His canon included the Epistles of St. Paul (excluding the Pastorals) and a greatly edited version of Luke's Gospel. The next canon is the fragment known as the Muratorian Canon, written around 170. While parts of it are missing, it lists as recognized Scripture the four Gospels, Matthew, Mark, Luke and John; Acts of the Apostles; Paul's Epistles, First and Second Corinthians, Ephesians, Philippians, Colossians, Galatians, First and Second Thessalonians, First and Second Timothy, Titus and Philemon; Epistle of Jude; First and Second John; Revelation. All authorities agree that the Epistle to the Hebrews, the Epistle of James and Second Peter were omitted from the canon.

Since the surviving document is incomplete, there is no way we can be sure what else was deliberately omitted from our present list of New Testament Books. E. J. Bicknell says that First Peter was included, and Second Peter was listed as doubtful:

> "The Muratorian Canon includes . . . the First Epistle of S. Peter. The Second Epistle of S. Peter is treated as doubtful. 'Some of the members do not wish it to be read in the church'" *(The Thirty-Nine Articles of the Church of England).*

On the other hand, William Barclay states of the Muratorian Canon:

> "The one surprise is the omission of First Peter." *(Introducing the Bible.)*

The Oxford Dictionary of the Christian Church agrees that both First and Second Peter are omitted. In any event, we see the development of a canon closely approaching our own. However, there were many objections to Hebrews, James, Second and Third John, Second Peter, and Revelation.

In the third century, Origen lists all of the present books of the New Testament except James and Jude. Of the rest, he is unsure of Second Peter, and also indicates that many still doubt the authenticity of Second and Third John.

Next we find Eusebius of Caesarea, writing in the first part of the fourth century. He divided the books of the New Testament (and other writings) into three classes: (1) acknowledged, (2) disputed, (3) spurious. Some of the New Testament he lists as disputed (e.g. James, Jude, Second and Third John, and Second Peter). He also lists Revelation in all three classes.

The canon of St. Cyril of Jerusalem (A.D. 340) includes all the New Testament except Revelation.

In 367, St. Athanasius issued an Easter letter to his people listing all twenty-seven Books of the New Testament as Holy Scripture:

> "There must be no hesitation to state again the books of the New Testament, for they are these: Four Gospels, according to Matthew, according to Mark, according to Luke and according to John. Further, after these, also the Acts of the Apostles, and the seven so-called Catholic Epistles of the Apostles, as follows: one of James, but two of Peter, then three of John, and after these one of Jude; in addition to these there are fourteen Epistles of the apostle Paul put down in the following order: the first to the Romans, then two to the Corinthians, and after these the Epistles to the Galatians, and then to the Ephesians: further, the Epistles to the Philippians and to the Colossians and two to the Thessalonians, and the Epistle to the Hebrews. And next two Letters to Timothy, but one to Titus, and the last one to Philemon. Moreover also, the Apocalypse of John" *(Festal Epistle, 39).*

The final canon of the New Testament was approved by the Synod of Carthage in 397. This action was recognized in Africa and Europe. A similar action was taken for the Eastern Church at the Trullan Synod in 692. From the seventh century on, the whole Christian Church has accepted the New Testament as we now know it. For this reason, Article VI says simply, "All the Books of the New Testament, as they are commonly received, we do receive, and account them Canonical."

While the whole Church finally agreed on the Books to be included in the New Testament canon, there were also Books which were seriously considered, but later excluded. Those tentatively included were First Clement (an Epistle to the Corinthians by Clement, Bishop of Rome, written in the last decade of the first century); Hermas (The Shepherd); the Apocalypse of Peter; and the Epistle of Barnabas. By the fourth century, these had been relegated to non-Scriptural but important writings. The final test for inclusion was whether the Book was recognized to bear the stamp of apostolic truth and to set forth the apostolic gospel. For this reason, authorship was limited to those who had seen Our Lord.

But what did the early Church think of Holy Scripture? Since the writing of that Scripture began in the first century, and continued into the opening decades of the second, let us begin with second century Fathers.

Irenaeus, writing around 180, and Tertullian writing at about the same time, or a little later (c. 200), both see Christ as the ultimate source of teaching and authority in the Church. However, that ultimate source is contained in both Scripture and Tradition. Irenaeus, for example, sees the apostolic tradition as residing both in the teaching passed on to the bishops (Spirit endowed men who have been vouchsafed "an infallible Charism of truth" *adv. haer.* 4, 26, 2) and deposited in written documents ("What the apostles at first proclaimed by word of mouth, they afterwards by God's will conveyed to us in Scriptures" *adv. haer.* 3, 1, 1,).

Tertullian, writing in his work, *Of Heretical Prescriptions* (De praescr. 21), says much the same that Ireneaus said above in his work, *Against Heresies*. Tertullian stated that tradition was enshrined in Scripture, for the apostles subsequently wrote down their oral preaching in epistles.

In the next two centuries, with the canon of the New Testament becoming more and more fixed, we find a more direct reference to Scripture as the final authority of the Church.

Origen, writing in the middle of the third century, stated:

"If any thing remains which Holy Scripture does not determine, no other third scripture ought to be received to authorize any knowledge, but we must commit to the fire what remains, that is, reserve it unto God" *(Hom. V. in Lev.).*

Athanasius, writing a hundred years later, said:

"The holy and divinely-inspired Scriptures are of themselves sufficient to the enunciation of the truth" *(Contra Gentes*, 1.).

Cyril of Jerusalem, writing c. 350, in his 24 Catecheses, said:

"With regard to the divine and saving mysteries of faith no doctrine, however trivial, may be taught without the backing of the divine Scriptures .... For our saving faith derives its force, not from capricious reasonings, but from what may be proved out of the Bible" (Cat. 4.).

And again, Athanasius says of Scripture:

"In these alone the doctrine of salvation is contained. Let no man add to or take from them"*(Festal Epistles*, ii.).

A few years later, Basil wrote of the Bible:

"Believe those things that are written: the things which are not written, seek not" *(Hom.* 29.).

In the early fifth century, Augustine of Hippo wrote:

"In those things which are plainly laid down in Scripture, all things are found, which embrace faith and morals" *(De doct. christ.* 2.).

A few decades after Augustine's statement, we come to the touchstone of St. Vincent of Lerins, written in his *Commonitorium*. Again, we find that balance between Scripture and Tradition which we saw in the second century:

"We said above that this has always been, and even at this day is, the custom of Catholics to try and examine the true faith by these two methods: first, by the authority of the divine canon (i.e. Scripture); secondly, by the rule of the Catholic Church (i.e. Tradition); not because the canonical Scripture is not as to itself sufficient for all things, but because very many, expounding God's word at their own will, do thereby conceive divers opinions and errors. And for this cause it is necessary that the interpretation of the heavenly Scripture be directed according to the one only rule of the Church's understanding; only, be it observed, especially in those questions upon which the foundations of the whole Catholic doctrine depend."

This twofold authority of Bible and Tradition is seen in the Articles of Religion. Again returning to Article VI, we read:

"Holy Scripture containeth all things necessary to salvation: so that whatsoever is not read therein, nor may be proved thereby, is not to be required of any man, that it should be believed as an article of the Faith, or be thought requisite or necessary to salvation."

Thus, Scripture is the primary authority.

On the other hand, the Church also has authority as witness and keeper of Holy Scripture. As Article XX says:

"The Church hath ... authority in Controversies of Faith; and yet it is not lawful for the Church to ordain any thing that is contrary to God's Word written, neither may it so expound one place of Scripture, that it be repugnant to another. Wherefore, although the Church be a witness and keeper of Holy Writ, yet, as it ought not to decree any thing against the same, so besides the same ought it not to enforce any thing to be believed for necessity of Salvation."

That position, first set forth in the second century, and reaffirmed by the Articles in the sixteenth, is still the position of the Anglican Communion in the twentieth. As Francis J. Hall, outstanding twentieth century Anglican theologian, said:

"(W)e should seek to ascertain that which is taught by the Catholic Church as necessary to be believed for salvation, and is contained in the Sacred Scriptures; for such doctrine, and such only, constitutes the necessary faith of Christians. It can be seen that our knowledge of saving doctrine is based upon an acceptance of the authority of both the Catholic Church and the Bible. These two are necessarily in agreement, since the teaching of both comes from the same divine source.

"But the manner in which the rule of faith requires us to depend upon the authority of the Church on the one hand, and of Holy Scripture on the other, is somewhat different. The Church is commissioned and guided by God to teach and define the faith. It is from her, therefore, that we learn its precise contents. On the other hand, all saving truth has by divine inspiration been imbedded in manifold ways in the Scriptures; and by their use we are able to verify, and enrich our hold upon, the truths which the Church teaches and defines. To put the matter summarily, the Church teaches and defines, while the Bible confirms and illustrates, everything that is necessary to be believed. Nothing may be held that contradicts catholic doctrine, and nothing may be required to be believed as necessary for salvation that is not contained in the Scriptures." (Hall, *Authority, Ecclesiastical and Biblical,* Vol. II, Dogmatic Theology.)

We might paraphrase this in the words of an old aphorism oft quoted: *"The Church to teach, the Bible to prove."*

If the Bible, then, is the final foundation upon which the Faith depends, what do we mean when we speak of Scripture as being "inspired"? The Christian religion is a revealed religion. Its original source is prophecy, not philosophy. The preachers of the Christian religion do not offer men a new philosophy, they offer them the "good news" that the Son of God is come into the world, and has risen from the dead. Christianity is the result of God's revelation of himself to us in the life, death and resurrection of Jesus Christ.

As C. B. Moss said, in his great work, *The Christian Faith:*

"God's method of revelation was to choose one particular people, who should receive His message, and in due time pass it on to the rest of mankind . . . .

"But God did not reveal Himself, even to the Hebrews, all at once. The Old Testament is the history of that revelation: 'God spake by many portions and in many manners to the fathers by the prophets' (Heb. i. 1) . . . .

"The revelation of God to the prophets, psalmists, sages, and seers of the Old Testament was the preparation for the full revelation of God in Jesus Christ . . . .

"Our Lord Jesus Christ is 'the effulgence of the glory, and the very image of the person' of the Father (Heb. i. 3); 'in

Him dwelleth all the fulness of the Godhead bodily'. He is the Word of God (St. John i. 1, 14) in the fullest sense. In Him we see all of God that it is possible for man to see.

"Therefore there can be no further revelation. We do not believe that God has added, or ever will add, anything to His revelation in His Son.

* * *

"The revelation of God has to be written down; the record of it is found in the collection of books which we call the Bible, the 'Canon' of Holy Scripture . . . .

"The Bible is not revelation, but the record of it . . . . We believe that the writers of it were given a special kind of Divine guidance, which is called Inspiration; and that those who drew up the Canon or list of the books were also given special Divine guidance, to include these books and no other."

This is what we mean by revelation and inspiration. The books of the Bible are not "inspiring and therefore inspired"; they are the recorded Word of God. They are the record of God's revelation of himself to us.

Turning to the Report of the Commission on Christian Doctrine entitled *Doctrine in the Church of England*, we read the official position of the Church on the matter of Inspiration:

"The Bible is more than a collection of utterances, some of which are 'inspiring and therefore inspired.' It makes its special appeal partly in virtue of its unity as a whole. This unity consists in the "presentation of a self-revelation of God through history and experience—a self-revelation which develops in relation both to the response and to the resistance of man to the Divine initiative, and which culminates in the Incarnation.

Thus the theme of the Bible as a whole is GOD, though the working out of this theme is in parts obscure. At times the limitations of the human writer and his age distort for us the presentation of this central theme, as when vindictiveness is attributed to God; but the theme itself is never wholly obscured, and in its completeness the Bible produces the conviction that it is not only about God but that it is of God. God speaks to men through the Bible, which may therefore be rightly called 'the Word of God.'

From the Christian standpoint the Bible is unique, as being the inspired record of a unique revelation. It is the record of the special preparation for Christ, and of His direct impact upon men, through His life, Death, and Resurrection. It sets before us that historical movement of Divine self-disclosure of which the Gospel is the crown.

* * *

Hitherto we have been mainly concerned with the grounds on which we recognize the Inspiration of the Bible rather than with the nature of that Inspiration itself. Here we have first to remember that the books of the Bible, though received as the oracles of God, were written within, and accepted as canonical by, a living and worshipping society. They can only be fully understood in relation to that society and its life. Moreover, the Bible is the work of many writers — original authors, editors, and revisers — and its final form is due to the selective judgment of the Jewish and Christian Churches. It is in the process as a whole that we recognize the working of the Divine Spirit.

The Inspiration of the Bible as a whole, or of any particular book within it, may consist either in the inspiration of individual authors or in the inspiration of those who selected, interpreted, and used already existing material. If it is contended that the latter were divinely guided rather than inspired, we would reply — first, that this distinction between God's ways of working upon or through the minds of men cannot ultimately be maintained, but also that even if it could the term Inspiration would rightly be retained for work which is truly creative, though it incorporates material already in existence.

Inspiration is not to be thought of as analogous to 'possession,' in which the personality of the possessed is superseded; nor does it appear that its nature can be illustrated by reference to those 'psychical phenomena' which have recently attracted great interest in many quarters. The truly inspired are those whose response to the Spirit of God has issued in a free surrender to His guidance. In this surrender all individual characteristics of mentality, temperament, knowledge, and the like remain, and when Inspiration issues in writing these characteristics appear in what is written."

While quite long, the above quotation states, in official language, and in clear terms, precisely what the Church believes in regard to the inspiration of Holy Scripture. We are therefore brought back to the familiar saying, "the Church to teach, the Bible to prove." As we look at the teaching of the Church in the following chapters, we will see more clearly the role of the Bible in proving the teaching of the Church.

PART II

The Creeds

Article VIII of the Articles of Religion states:

"The Nicene Creed, and that which is commonly called the Apostles' Creed, ought thoroughly to be received and believed; for they may be proved by most certain warrants of Holy Scripture."

In chapter 2, we will be examining the historical controversies out of which the theology of the Church developed in regard to questions of the Nature of God, the Holy Trinity, the Incarnation and the Person of Jesus Christ, as well as the Church. It is from those controversies that the theological developments led to the formulation of the Creeds.

However, the Creeds are always rooted in Scripture, as Article VIII so aptly says. Chapter 3, in particular, will trace the Biblical authority for the articles of the Creeds.

CHAPTER 2

The Holy Trinity, The Incarnation, and the Church

"Hear, O Israel, the Lord Your God is One God."
"I believe in One God . . . "

The cry of ancient Israel, and the credal statement of faith of the Christian are the same; there is only one God. The concept of one God is not limited, however, to Jewish or Christian theology. The Greek philosophers had arrived at the conclusion that the Power beyond and behind the universe had to be One. Socrates, Plato, Aristotle and many others looked to the One God underlying the polytheism of their day. Whether it be described as the prime force or element predating all else or whether it be called the "unknowable divine," there was in ancient philosophy blind groping toward the truth that God is One. In the face of this, however, the Christian speaks of God the Father, God the Son, and God the Holy Ghost. Does Christianity then teach three Gods, while pretending to believe in only one?

These are the questions which have faced men from the beginning of the Christian revelation. These are the questions which will shape the very structure of belief and which have led to the theology of the Holy Trinity. As with all questions concerning the relationship of God and man and the nature and purpose of God, we must start with Holy Scripture. Scripture tells us:

(1) there is One God:

(a) "Hear, O Israel: The Lord Our God is the only Lord" (Mk. xii. 29).

(b) "I am the Lord, and there is none else, there is no God beside me" (Isa. xlv. 5).

(c) "There is no God but one" (I Cor. viii. 4).

(d) "There is . . . one God and Father of all . . ."(Eph. iv. 4, 6).

(e) "Before me there was no god fashioned nor ever shall be after me. I am the Lord, I myself . . . I am the first and the last, and there is no god but me" (Isa. xliii. 10, 11; xliv. 7).

(2) The Father is God:

(a) "God the Father has set the seal of his authority" (Jn. vi. 27).

(b) "God is our father, and God alone" (Jn. viii. 41).

(c) " . . . one God and Father for all . . . " (Eph. iv. 6).

(d) " . . . for us there is one God, the Father . . . " (I Cor. viii. 6).

(e) "(Y)ou say 'Our Father' to the one who judges every man . . . " (I Pet. i. 17).

(f) "(A)t the hands of God the Father he was invested with honour and glory . . . " (II Pet. i. 17).

(3) The Son is God:

(a) "In the beginning was the Word, and the Word was with God, and the Word was God . . . the Word became flesh and dwelt among us" (Jn. i. 1, 14).

(b) "Jesus . . . said to Thomas, 'Reach your finger here . . . Be unbelieving no longer, but believe.' Thomas said, 'My Lord and my God' " (Jn. xx. 27, 28).

(c) "And the men fell at (Jesus') feet exclaiming, 'Truly you are the son of God' " (Matt. xiv. 33).

(d) " . . . he said he was God's son" (Matt. xxvii. 43).

(e) "Jesus said, 'In very truth I tell you, before Abraham was born, I am' " (Jn. viii. 58). (See Ex. iii. 13, 14: "Then Moses said to God, 'If I go to the Israelites and tell them that God . . . has sent me . . . and they ask me His name, what shall I say?' God answered, 'I am; that is who I am. Tell them that I AM has sent you to them.' ")

(4) The Holy Spirit is God:

(a) "In the beginning of Creation, when God made heaven and earth, the earth was without form and void, with darkness over the face of the abyss, and the Spirit of God hovered over the surface of the waters" (Gen. i. 1, 2).

(b) "He saw the Spirit of God descending like a dove . . ." (Matt. iii. 16).

(c) "All who are moved by the Spirit of God are sons of God. . . . The Spirit of God joins with our spirit in testifying that we are God's children" (Rom. viii. 14, 16).

(d) "For the Spirit explores everything, even the depths of God's own nature. Among men, who knows what a man is but the man's own spirit within him? In the same way, only the Spirit of God knows what God is. This is the Spirit that we have received from God . . . " (I Cor. ii. 10-12).

(e) "But when your Advocate has come, whom I will send you from the Father — the Spirit of Truth that issues from the Father — he will bear witness to me . . . when he comes who is the Spirit of Truth, he will guide you into all truth" (Jn. xv. 26; xvi. 13).

(f) "(W)hoever slanders the Holy Spirit can never be forgiven; he is guilty of eternal sin" (Mk. iii. 29).

(g) "God himself ransomed them . . . yet they rebelled and grieved his Holy Spirit" (Isa. lxiii. 9, 10).

(5) The Three (Father, Son and Holy Spirit) are one:

(a) "Baptize men everywhere in the name of the Father and the Son and the Holy Spirit . . . " (Matt. xxviii. 19).

(The Name is one. It belongs equally to the three Persons, who are associated on an equality.)

(b) "(Jesus said) My Father and I are one" (Jn. x. 30).

(c) "The grace of the Lord Jesus Christ, and the love of God, and fellowship in the Holy Spirit, be with you all" (II Cor. xiii. 14).

(d) "For there are three that bear record in heaven, the Father, the Word, and the Holy Ghost: and these three are one" (I Jn. v. 7).

Thus, we see One God, of Three Persons, the Father, Son and Holy Spirit. Scripture further tells us that the Son is begotten of the Father before all creation (Jn. i. l; Col. i. 17), and that the Holy Spirit, also existing before all creation (Gen. i. l), proceeds from the Father, through the Son (Jn. xv. 26). It is this which is the basis of our understanding of the Holy Trinity. However, many persons attempted to explain the revelation of God in terms of a given culture without proper safeguard for the ultimate truth of God's Being.

The earliest Christians were Jews, and thought in Hebrew or Aramaic, taking for granted the revelation of God to the Hebrew prophets. But as soon as they began to preach to the Gentiles, the more educated of whom had been trained in Greek philosophy, they had to give their message in a Greek form. This increased the possibility of a misunderstanding, or even an imperfect explanation. These imperfect explanations, as is so often the case, grasped one phase or facet of the truth, and denied all else. The result is a lop-sided version of the situation.

The Church began to define and develop the doctrine of the Holy Trinity only in response to the *untrue* statements made. The Church had no intention of attempting to define the nature of God, and indeed, we humans simply cannot fully comprehend God. If we begin with this realization — that God is beyond our ability to comprehend, only then can we begin to explain what we DO know and understand about him.

The way we see life, the way we live, and the basis for our whole approach to life, is rooted ultimately in our belief about God. If we believe in a personal God, who has entered into human history, and has shared our own lot in life, then we will live and relate to others around us in a certain way. If we believe in an impersonal God, who cannot be approached, and who cannot (or will not) enter into the fabric of human history, then we react to life in an entirely different manner. Therefore, it becomes extremely important that we do define and study what we can say about the very nature of God, especially when we are speaking in response to one-sided views which do not square with the revelation of God in Holy Scripture. When we speak of the doctrine of God, we must refer both to the truth of the Trinity, and the place of Jesus in the revelation of God.

Those attempts to develop a doctrine of God which are untruths, or heresies, fall roughly into two groups: those who deny the real entrance of God into human experience, and those who deny the reality of human experience to God.

The first group includes the Ebionites. These people attempted to explain Jesus in the framework of Jewish thought, and to preserve the Unity of God by denying the divinity of Jesus. Jesus was a "good man," a prophet, and a great teacher, but he was not God. Ebionites regarded the idea of a real Incarnation as blasphemous. It was unthinkable that the high and Holy God could degrade himself by appearing in human form on earth. Further, to suppose that Jesus Christ was God endangered the Unity of God. Jesus could, at most, be a new prophet or law-giver, a second Moses, sent not to replace, but to fulfill the law. Christians were to obtain salvation by a right observance of the Law as interpreted by him.

The second group includes the followers of Docetism. These people attempted to explain the Christ in the framework of Gentile dualism. God is good, and matter is evil. Therefore the Christ is truly God, but he is not really human or physical. He had only the appearance of humanity. For entirely different reasons, Docetists, like the Ebionites, found a real Incarnation unthinkable. The good God could never pollute himself by entering into union with matter. Men needed a Saviour who would free them from bondage to matter. So the physical side of Our Lord's life, his birth, eating and drinking, and of course his death, must all be only an appearance. His Body must be only a phantom. If men need only to be enlightened by the revealed truth about God and themselves, a Docetic Christ would answer all requirements. An "appearance" can supply the picture of God and redemption.

The fallacy of each viewpoint is apparent when we examine the logical consequences of each position. If Jesus is not God, then God does not really know how we feel; he does not really know the meaning of human suffering, and he does not really love us to the point of being born in our world, and dying, even as we must die. Thus, we have no revelation of the Love of God for us.

If Jesus is not man, then our humanity is not saved by the death and resurrection of Christ. The world, which God made, is itself dirty and evil, and beyond any real salvation. Moreover, the so-called Passion of Our Lord, his Sacrifice on the Cross, and the glory of his Resurrection and Ascension, are all a form of cruel hoax.

Applying these consequences to the Trinity, we see that each bears on the question of whether there be only One Person or more than One Person in the Godhead. The New Testament assumes that there is only One God, and yet teaches that the Father, Son and Holy Spirit are equally divine. The one-sided theories formed to explain this may, again, be divided into two classes: Those which make too little of the distinction between the Persons and those which make too much of it.

The first class treats the difference between the Persons as unreal, and emphasizes the Unity of God by denying any distinctions with the Godhead. One example of this class is a tongue-twister called "Modalistic Monarchianism". Modalistic Monarchianism is the belief that one God exists in two or three modes. As Father, he created; as Son, he redeemed the world; as Holy Spirit, he sanctifies. However, these are simply modes or facets of a single Being or Person. This theory was put forth by such men as Praxeas and Noetus in the second century. A later development of this belief was "Sabellianism," so named because it was taught by a third century Roman Priest, Sabellius. Sabellianism taught that the Eternal Being (apparently regarded as impersonal) existed in three forms: Father, Son and Holy Spirit. This impersonal God had expanded to create the universe, and again to redeem mankind, but at the end of the ages, it would contract again and the distinction between the modes of being would no longer exist.

The second class tends to treat the unity between Persons as less than complete, and emphasizes, instead, the distinction between the Persons. The most extreme example is Tritheism — the belief in three separate Gods. This theory is

THE HOLY TRINITY, THE INCARNATION, AND THE CHURCH   41

so violently contrary to the clear Biblical teaching of the Unity of God that hardly anyone went so far as to teach Tritheism. However, in the sixth century, one John Philoponos, a leader of the Monophysite heresy actually taught belief in three Gods. The followers of Marcion, called Marcionites, saw Christ as a personal, knowable emanation from the unknowable God, and as a separate Being. The most important of all these theories was that of Arius, a priest at Alexandria. Arianism developed from the views of Paul of Samosata. Paul taught that Jesus was a man who, for his great virtue and merit, received the Word of God, and was adopted into the Godhead. Arius denied the possibility of a real Incarnation. He regarded the Unity of God in such a way as to exclude all contact between God and the world. Accordingly, he endeavored to find a place for Christ outside the being of God, yet above creation. Thus, the Father is God, but the Son is a demi-god; two different Beings, of two different substances.

The first of these theories, by denying the separate Persons of the Trinity, denies that God is Love. The New Testament clearly represents the Father and the Son as loving each other. Two aspects or modes of one person cannot feel love for one another. Modalism (and Sabellianism) was rightly felt to be inconsistent with the evidence of the Gospels.

The other class of theories is equally faulty, as they deny the essential Unity of God, and, at least by implication, deny the true divinity of Christ. This is also clearly contrary to New Testament Scripture. Thus, all the heresies failed to present in human terms the concept of God as revealed in the Scriptures and human experience.

The Church, then, had to make statements of doctrine, in response to the viewpoints raised in error or ignorance. Perhaps the best known attempt to explain, in some degree, the Holy Trinity was that made by St. Patrick, when the pagan Irish asked him the same question which still troubles people. As St. Patrick was preaching the Christian Faith, he was asked how he could assert the fact that there was only One God, when at the same time he referred over and over again not only to Our Father (who is God), but also to God the Son and God the Holy Spirit. "Aren't you really saying that there are Three Gods?", people demanded. "How can you mention three Persons, and then say there is only one God?"

Patrick answered by plucking a shamrock, and holding it

up for the people to see. He pointed out that although the shamrock had three distinct parts, which at first appeared to be three separate leaves, the plant was one, with only one leaf. "Just as the shamrock has three parts, but is one plant," he said, "so God is three Persons, but is only One God."

Patrick was only trying to put in symbolic language both the Scriptural teaching and our own experience. A very good example of personal experience was described in Volume III of the first Church's Teaching Series, *The Faith of the Church*, in chapter 12. We are told that a young Roman citizen living in the second century had been noticing that a remarkable change had occurred in the life of a friend of long standing. He was seen with a set of acquaintances drawn from every level of society. About the time the young citizen was ready to ask some questions, he found that his friend was eager to tell him of his new faith. As a result, they set off to attend one of the meetings of this new group, in an obscure part of the city.

While the visitor did not understand much of what was being said or done in the meeting, it became apparent to him that this group of men and women were of one mind, and were dominated by an *esprit de corps*, indeed a *holy* esprit, or Holy Spirit. Already, the visitor was beginning to know the fellowship of the Holy Spirit. This new experience, this Holy Spirit, brought him back again and again. He began to learn more and more about one Jesus. He found that the group was called Christian, because the members were Christ's men. He learned of Jesus as a personal, loving Lord and Saviour. As he learned more about Jesus, he learned about the Father who had sent Jesus, who created and creates the world and all in it. He was able to identify the Father with the God, supreme in immensity, majesty and creativity, the God of philosophy. But now he learned that this God willed to be in personal relationship with his human creatures, and had made this relationship possible through Christ. Thus, the young Roman had experienced God in three ways. As the authors of Volume III said:

> "The order of experience for him, as for many Christians, is the Holy Ghost, the Son and the Father."

This is the Holy Trinity as we experience it. How does the Church define this experience, in the light of Scripture, and in response to heretical viewpoints?

One of our earliest writers and authorities was St. Clement of Rome. Toward the end of the first century, he wrote his *First Epistle to the Corinthians*. In chapter 46, Clement uses the Trinitarian formula, when he asks, "Have we not one God (the Father) and one Christ and one Spirit?" Again, in chapter 58, Clement writes, "God liveth, and the Lord Jesus liveth, and the Holy Spirit, who are the faith and hope of the elect."

Half a century later, the *Didache* (or "Teaching of the Twelve Apostles"), in chapter 7, set forth the form for Baptism. Here again, we see the very clearcut Triune Name of God, for Baptism is "In the Name of the Father and of the Son and of the Holy Spirit."

The term "Trinity" first appeared in A.D. 180, when Theophilus of Antioch, in speaking of God, his Word and his Wisdom, used the Greek word "trias." A few years later, Tertullian, in his work, *Adversus Praxeam*, in refuting Modalistic Monarchianism, used the Latin equivalent "Trinitas." He was also the first to use the terms "Una Substantia, Tres Personae" ("One Substance, three Persons"). In chapter 29, he writes:

> "The mystery of the providential order which arranges the Unity in a Trinity, setting in their order three — Father, Son, and Holy Spirit — three, however, not in condition but in relation, and not in substance but in mode of existence, and not in power, but in special characteristics."

Una Substantia asserts in uncompromising fashion the Unity of God. The term "persona" was employed by Tertullian in the sense in which we speak of first, second and third persons in the conjugation of a verb. He regarded the Persons of the Trinity as holding converse with one another or speaking in reference to one another. These terms commended themselves to the Western Church. During the Arian controversy the West was strongly orthodox, largely because it had already been provided with language in which to express the relations of the "One" and the "Three."

In the East agreement was less quickly reached. Part of the problem was the use of the Greek word *ousia*. The terms used were *mia ousia* (Una Substantia) and *treis hypostaseis* (Tres Personae). However, *ousia* had two meanings, one of which was a common essence of being (substance), and the other, an individual being (person). On the other hand, *hypostasis* while also a synonym (originally) for *ousia*, was a less common word, and as a technical term, came to mean "person." This meant that *ousia* would be interpreted as "substance."

The Council of Nicea had used the term *homoousios* in the Creed *(homo* = same; *ousia* = substance). Yet with the confusion of the meaning of *ousia*, this might mean the same person (Sabellianism), or with *hypostasis* as a synonym, *treis hypostaseis* could mean Three Substances (Tritheism or Arianism).

The problem was finally resolved at the Council of Alexandria in the last half of the fourth century. Gradually, the usage of the Church settled down to the formula, *mia ousia kai treis hypostaseis* in the East, which was equal to *Una Substantia et Tres Personae* in the West. In English we speak about "Three Persons in One Substance."

Perhaps one of the earliest clearcut statements of the doctrine of the Holy Trinity is the Athanasian Creed. Dating from the late fourth century, it states:

> "And the Catholic Faith is this: That we worship one God in Trinity, and Trinity in Unity; neither confounding the Persons; nor dividing the substance. For there is one Person of the Father, another of the Son, and another of the Holy Ghost.
>
> But the Godhead of the Father, of the Son, and of the Holy Ghost, is all one; the glory equal, the majesty co-eternal. Such as the Father is, such is the Son, and such is the Holy Ghost.
>
> The Father uncreate, the Son uncreate, and the Holy Ghost uncreate: The Father incomprehensible, the Son incomprehensible, and the Holy Ghost incomprehensible: The Father eternal, the Son eternal, and the Holy Ghost eternal. And yet they are not three eternals, but one eternal; as also there are not three incomprehensibles, nor three uncreated, but one uncreated and one incomprehensible.
>
> So likewise the Father is almighty, the Son almighty, and the Holy Ghost almighty. And yet they are not three almighties, but one almighty. So the Father is God, the Son is God, and the Holy Ghost is God. And yet they are not three Gods, but one God. So likewise the Father is

Lord, the Son is Lord, and the Holy Ghost Lord. And yet not three Lords, but one Lord.

For like as we are compelled by the Christian verity to acknowledge every Person by himself to be God and Lord, so are we forbidden by the Catholic Religion to say, there be three Gods, or three Lords.

The Father is made of none, neither created nor begotten. The Son is of the Father alone, not made, nor created, but begotten. The Holy Ghost is of the Father and of the Son, neither made nor created, nor begotten, but proceeding.

So there is one Father, not three Fathers; one Son, not three Sons; one Holy Ghost, not three Holy Ghosts.

And in this Trinity none is afore or after other, none is greater or less than another. But the whole three Persons are co-eternal together, and co-equal; So that in all things, as is aforesaid, the Unity in Trinity, and the Trinity in Unity is to be worshipped."

St. Augustine of Hippo saw the Holy Trinity as essential to the concept of God as Love, and God as a Unity. "Love," he said, "is of someone that loves, and with love someone is loved. Behold then there are three things: he that loves, that which is loved, and love itself" *(De Trinitate)*.

The same concept is expressed in a more vivid fashion by Dom Gregory Dix, the great Anglican Benedictine scholar:

"Ever in the Holy Trinity, the Father gives Himself to the Son and the Son to the Father in a torrent of love which is the Holy Ghost. The whole perfect Being of God passes eternally from one to another and returns in an unending dance of love — the perfect love of the perfect lover for the perfectly beloved, perfectly achieved and perfectly returned forever. That is the life of God Himself in the eternal abyss of His own Being. It is love and it is joy, illimitable joy" *(The Power of God)*.

The Prayer Book and the Articles of Religion speak of the Holy Trinity, both in the language of the Church, and in the language of human experience. The First Article of Religion is entitled, "Of Faith in the Holy Trinity," and says:

"There is but one living and true God, everlasting, without body, parts, or passions; of infinite power, wisdom, and goodness; the Maker, and Preserver of all things both visible and invisible. And in unity of this Godhead there be three Persons, of one substance, power and eternity; the Father, the Son, and the Holy Ghost."

In the First Office of Instruction of the 1928 Prayer Book, we say:

"First I learn to believe in God the Father, who hath made me, and all the world.

"Secondly, in God the Son, who hath redeemed me, and all mankind.

"Thirdly, in God the Holy Ghost, who sanctifieth me, and all the people of God."

The revelation of God in Holy Scripture and the experience of human living are fully explained only in the light of the doctrine of the Holy Trinity, as expressed in the statements of the Church. However, God the Holy Trinity, is complete within himself. And thus the question arises, how *do* we bridge the gap that appears to exist between the world and God?

The answer is that we do not bridge the gap, but that God does. Throughout the Old Testament, we have example after example of God revealing himself to men; of God entering into history by way of the prophets. These revelations, however, are not total, final or complete. They only prepare the way for the final act of revelation — the Incarnation.

Just as Scripture spoke to us about the Holy Trinity, so it speaks to us about the Person of Jesus Christ.

As we saw earlier, in the section on the Holy Trinity, Jesus Christ is God (Jn. i. 1; Jn. xx. 28; Matt. xiv. 33; Matt. xxvii. 43).

If Jesus be God, can he also be man? Scripture tells us:

(1) Jesus grew in body, mind and soul:

(a) "The child grew big and strong and full of wisdom" (Lk. ii. 40).

b) "Because of his humble submission his prayer was heard. Son though he was, he learned obedience in the

THE HOLY TRINITY, THE INCARNATION, AND THE CHURCH

school of suffering, and, once perfected, became the source of eternal salvation for all who obey him" (Heb. v. 7).

(2) He had purely human needs of hunger, thirst, weariness, etc.:

(a) "For forty days and nights he fasted, and at the end of them, he was famished" (Matt. iv. 2).

(b) "Now he was in the stern asleep on the cushion" (Mk. iv. 38).

(c) "It was about noon, and Jesus, tired after his journey, sat down by the well" (Jn. iv. 6).

(d) "Jesus said . . . I thirst" (Jn. xix. 28).

(3) He had human emotions of anger, wonder, sorrow, etc.:

(a) "they had nothing to say; and, looking round at them with anger and sorrow at their obstinate stupidity, he said to the man, 'Stretch out your arm' " (Mk. iii. 5).

(b) "(H)e was taken aback by their want of faith" (Mk. vi. 6).

(c) "Horror and dismay came over him, and he said to them, 'My heart is ready to break with grief' . . . " (Mk. xiv. 33, 34).

(d) "When Jesus heard this, he admired the man . . . " (Lk. vii. 9).

(e) "When Jesus saw her weeping and the Jews her companions weeping, he sighed heavily and was deeply moved" (Jn. xi. 33).

(4) He prayed and exhibited a true human faith in the Father:

(a) "He went away to a lonely spot and remained there in prayer" (Mk. i. 35).

(b) "Then Jesus looked upwards and said, 'Father, I thank thee; thou hast heard me' " (Jn. xi. 41, 42).

(5) He was tempted and experienced the trials of uncertainty:

(a) "Then he ... prayed that, if it were possible, this hour might pass him by. 'Abba, Father,' he said, 'All things are possible to thee; take this cup from me'" (Mk. xiv. 35, 36).

(b) "Jesus was then led away by the Spirit into the wilderness to be tempted by the devil" (Matt. iv. i.).

(c) "For since he himself has passed through the test of suffering, he is able to help those who are meeting their test now" (Heb. ii. 18).

(6) He could be disappointed and disobeyed:

(a) "Then he dismissed him with this stern warning: 'Be sure you say nothing to anybody ...' But the man went out and made the whole story public" (Mk. i. 43-45).

(b) "He said to them, 'Why are you such cowards? Have you no faith even now?'" (Mk. iv. 40).

(7) He asked questions for the sake of information and confessed to ignorance on at least one point:

(a) "Jesus asked his father, 'How long has he been like this?' 'From childhood,' he replied" (Mk. ix. 21).

(b) "(H)e felt hungry, and noticing in the distance a fig-tree in leaf, he went to see if he could find anything on it" (Mk. xi. 13).

(c) "'Where have you laid him?' he asked" (Jn. xi. 34).

(d) "But about that day or that hour no one knows, not even the angels in heaven, not even the Son; only the Father" (Mk. xiii. 32).

We can thus see that Jesus Christ is both God and Man. While being both God and man, he was, nevertheless, one Person. His life was in all ways a unity. And yet, controversy still remained. The point at issue was no longer whether he was "of one substance with the Father"—but the relation between his divinity and his humanity. How could Jesus Christ be both the Eternal Son and also truly man?

The doctrine of the Incarnation is simply the belief that, in the words of the Prologue to John's Gospel, "In the beginning was the Word, and the Word was with God, and the Word was God . . . and the Word became flesh and dwelt among us" — that is, God the Son, the Second Person of the Trinity, took human nature.

Just as the teaching concerning the Holy Trinity caused great difficulty, so the teaching concerning the Incarnation has caused much confusion. We saw, in the discussion on the Holy Trinity, the problems raised by Arianism. This controversy actually split the Church for some time. When the Arian movement began, the persecutions were just over. The "New Rome," or Constantinople, had become the center of political and religious power. Constantine had tried to unite the Empire around the Christian Church, and this meant a unity of doctrine. However, the Emperor was not so much concerned with *truth* as he was with *unity*. Two of the most important cities of the Empire (after Rome and Constantinople) were Alexandria and Antioch. Each had its own theological school, which represented one particular tendency in human thought. The rivalry between these schools, carried to final conclusion, produced opposite heresies.

Arius had been a parish priest in Alexandria, but was from Antioch. He had been educated in the Antiochean school which emphasized the humanity of Jesus whereas the school at Alexandria emphasized the divinity of Christ. Arius ran into trouble with the Archbishop of Alexandria, Alexander, for teaching that God was not always Father, but only became so when he created the Son; that the Son was created, that once he did not exist, and that he was therefore unlike the Father in essence; that he was not the true Word of the Father; that he was created for the purpose of producing mankind; that he did not know perfectly either the Father or himself; and that, unlike the Father, he was liable to change.

For this teaching, Arius, two bishops, six other priests and six deacons were all excommunicated by a local council of Egyptian Bishops. Arius was given sanctuary by Eusebius, Bishop of Nicomedia. In order to settle the dispute, Constantine called the Council of Nicea in A.D. 325. The Council condemned Arius, and specifically held that Jesus Christ *is* "of one substance with the Father." Unfortunately, this did not end the dispute, because the word for "one substance" in

Greek *(homoousion)* was subject to a Sabellian interpretation. It was not until the clarification of *ousia* and *hypostasis* at the Council of Alexandria that this problem was resolved.

A very unfortunate side effect of the Arian argument was the rise of Apollinarianism. Apollinarius, Bishop of Laodicea, had been a vigorous opponent of the Arians and a supporter of the Alexandrian school. He held that if the Lord's humanity were complete, we should have to suppose that he possessed two wills, one divine and infallible, the other human and free to sin. There could be no union between two such wills without the violation of the nature of one of them, and since the rational will is the directing principle in a person, the possession of two wills would destroy the unity of the Incarnate. Christ therefore had no human mind, to be the seat of rational deliberation and choice. His mind and will were those of the Divine Word; at the Incarnation, the Word took only a human body and an animal soul. There was no human mind or spirit. Apollinarius believed that this was the only way the unity of his person and the sinlessness of his will could be understood.

This viewpoint of Apollinarius contradicted many of the facts of Our Lord's earthly life. It can be shown from Scripture that in Christ the three ways in which humans act — the will, mind and feelings (called in the Bible the heart, mind and soul) — were all human. (For example, as to the humanity of his will, mind and feeling, see Mk. xiv. 56; Lk. ii. 52; Jn. xi. 36.) Appollinarius' theory left no room for growth in mind or soul and it abolished the possibility not only of sin, but of temptation.

Moreover, such a view regards human nature as unable to become the means of God's self-revelation. Not only does it regard the higher part of human nature as intrinsically sinful, but it leaves it unredeemed, and it is precisely this higher part which is most truly human. All that Christ assumed was the animal side of man. If what was not assumed was not redeemed, man's will, the ultimate seat of his being, was left unredeemed by Christ. Apollinarianism was condemned by the Council of Constantinople for this very reason. Apollinarianism was a reaction against Arianism. Arius had denied that the Son was in the full sense God, and Apollinarius denied that he was in the full sense man.

As a reaction from Apollinarianism there arose the heresy

know as Nestorianism. It, like Arianism, sprang from the school of Antioch. The leading representative of the school was Theodore, Bishop of Mopsuesta. Approaching the problem of the Person of Christ from the human side, he laid stress on the complete humanity of Our Lord. He taught that each of the two natures of Christ was personal. However, he held that the human nature was united to the Word by a kind of external tie, or conjunction of the two natures in Christ, not their union. This is compared to the union between man and wife, who are made one flesh.

Nestorius, a follower of Theodore, became Bishop of Constantinople in 428. He did little more than repeat the teachings of Theodore. However, in supporting one of his priests, Anastasius, Nestorius was driven to deny the title of *Theotokos* to denote the mother of Jesus. Nestorius denied the title to St. Mary on the ground that it suggests the divine nature of her Son was derived from her. The word means "God-Bearer," or "Mother of Him who is God." This meant to the Early Fathers (Origen, Chrysostom, et al.) not that Mary gave divinity to Jesus, but rather that he whom she bore was none other than the eternal Son of God.

The weakness of Nestorianism is that it reduces Our Lord to a superlatively inspired man, the Chief of the Saints. He is man side by side with God, not God in and through man. There is not unity of Person but concord of two Persons. To the contrary, we are compelled to state that Jesus Christ was God from the first moment of his existence as man. It was God incarnate who was born of Mary, and she is therefore rightly called Theotokos. Moreover, unless Jesus Christ had been God, and not merely a man united with God, he could not have redeemed us.

The next great heresy was Monophysitism. This heresy believed that Our Lord had but one nature, the Divine one. As Apollinarianism was a reaction against Arianism, and Nestorianism a reaction against Apollinarianism, so Monophysitism was a reaction against Nestorianism.

The school of Alexandria had come to represent a theology of Christ centered in his divinity, regarding his human life as a self manifestation of God in time. Cyril, Bishop of Alexandria, had used the expression "one nature of the Word of God, though this nature had assumed flesh." By this he meant that the Word of God in all the fulness of his divine nature had become personally incarnate. Further, he used the word "nature" as an equivalent of "person."

After the death of Cyril, Eutyches, an abbot at Constantinople, taught that Our Lord was of two natures before the union between them, but after the union only of one nature. He claimed that the Manhood of Christ was swallowed up in his Godhead, like a drop of vinegar in the ocean. Thus, Monophysite *(monos* = one; *physis* = nature). This opens the door to Docetism, and reduces Our Lord's humanity to a mere outward appearance. Eutyches was criticized by Leo of Rome, in a work entitled the "Tome of Leo," but won temporary support at the Robber Council of Ephesus. This decision was reversed by the Council of Chalcedon, which also approved the "Tome of Leo."

An attempt to reconcile the Monophysites to the Catholic view was made in the seventh century, by a position known as Monothelitism (from *monos* = one; *thelo* = I will). This position maintained that though Christ had two natures, yet these natures possessed or acted by but a single will. This leads us right back to Apollinarianism, and the position was condemned by the Council of Constantinople in 680.

Having seen this great variety of heresies and wrong views of the Incarnation, what then does the Church have to say about the doctrine?

Writing at the opening of the second century, Ignatius of Antioch directed a letter to the Church of Ephesus. In it (chapter 7) he used these phrases:

(a) "Son of Mary and Son of God." From the Blessed Virgin the incarnate Christ derived his human nature.

(b) "Generate and ingenerate." The human nature was "generate," being born of the Virgin Mary. The divine nature was "ingenerate", says Ignatius, for it existed before the Incarnation.

(c) "First passible and then impassible." The incarnate Christ as man could suffer. The risen, ascended, and glorified Christ can suffer no more, and so is impassible.

Ignatius goes on, in chapter 19, to speak of "Three mysteries to be cried aloud — the which were wrought in the silence of God." These three mysteries he describes as the Virgin Birth, the Incarnation and the Atonement. In his *Letter to Tralles*, Ignatius warns against the Docetists by stating that Christ is he "Who was truly born and ate and drank" (chapter 9). He therefore condemned those (Docetists) who taught "that he suffered only in semblance" on Calvary (chapter 10).

Hermas, writing *The Shepherd*, parable 9, chapter 12, says:

> "This rock and gate is the Son of God.... The Son of God is older than all His creation ... therefore also He is ancient ... He was made manifest in the last days of the consummation; therefore the gate was made recent."

We have here a doctrine of Our Lord's divine nature and office. God the Son is pre-existent, and the Agent of creation. He became incarnate in "the last days" to open the Kingdom of God to believers.

The most famous statement about the Incarnation is that of the Council of Nicea made in A.D. 325. It now comes down to us in the Nicene Creed:

> "We believe ... in one Lord Jesus Christ, the only-begotten Son of God; Begotten of his Father before all worlds, God of God, Light of Light, Very God of Very God; Begotten, not made; Being of one substance with the Father; By whom all things were made; Who for us men and for our salvation came down from heaven, and was incarnate by the Holy Ghost of the Virgin Mary, and was made man ... "

Even more explicitly, the Athanasian Creed speaks of the Incarnation:

> "Furthermore, it is necessary to everlasting salvation that he also believe rightly the Incarnation of Our Lord Jesus Christ. For the right faith is, that we believe and confess that Our Lord Jesus Christ, the Son of God, is God and man: God of the substance of the Father, begotten before the worlds; and man, of the substance of his Mother, born in the world.
>
> "Perfect God, and perfect man, of a reasonable soul and human flesh subsisting: Equal to the Father as touching his Godhead, and inferior to the Father as touching his manhood.

"Who, although he be God and man, yet he is not two, but one Christ. One, not by conversion of the Godhead into flesh, but by taking of the manhood into God.

"One altogether; not by confusion of substance, but by unity of person. For as the reasonable soul and flesh is one man, so God and man is one Christ."

Finally, the Church, in the Council of Chalcedon, A.D. 451, declared:

"Therefore following the holy Fathers, we confess and all with one consent teach men to confess one and the same Son, Our Lord Jesus Christ, the same perfect in Godhead and the same perfect in manhood, truly God and truly man, the same of a rational soul and body, of one substance with the Father according to His Godhead, and the same of one substance with us according to His manhood, in all things like to us, apart from sin, begotten of the Father before the ages according to His Godhead, and the same in the last days for us and for our salvation born of Mary the Virgin, Mother of God, according to His manhood, one and the same Christ, Son, Lord, Only-begotten, made known in two natures, without confusion, without conversion, without division, without separation, the difference of the natures having been in no way abolished through the union, but rather the property of each nature being preserved and meeting in one person and one hypostasis."

This is still the position of the Church, as set forth in the Second Article of Religion, entitled "Of the Word, or Son of God, Which was made very Man."

"The Son, which is the Word of the Father, begotten from everlasting of the Father, the very and eternal God, of one substance with the Father, took Man's nature in the womb of the blessed Virgin, of her substance: So that two whole and perfect natures, that is to say, the Godhood and Manhood were joined together in one Person, never to be divided, whereof is one Christ, very God, and very Man; who truly suffered, was crucified, dead and buried, to reconcile His Father to us, and to be a sacrifice, not only for original guilt, but also for all actual sins of men."

A final question we need to consider about the Incarnation is: What is the relationship between Christ and his Church? Where does the Church fit into this picture of the perfect God, who has bridged the gap between himself and the world in the person of Jesus Christ?

Just as there had been a special relationship between God and the Nation of Israel, so Our Lord has a special relationship with his followers. Jesus came not to destroy the law and prophetic vision of Israel but to fulfill and perfect it in himself. The Church, therefore, has a very special relation with Christ. She is an extension of Christ in the World and necessary for the work of God in the world.

Many people find difficulty in seeing any necessity for a Church at all. They regard religion as a purely personal and individual activity and recognize the utility of associations of like-minded people in order to effectively announce their teaching to whoever might accept them. But they see no need for a Christian community which is bound up with the Gospel entrusted to it in such a way that to accept the Gospel in its fullness must involve membership in that community. The nature of man is inherently social and man is constantly involved in the development of some form of community life. The essentially social nature of man and of the sin of man calls for social redemption, the establishing of a fellowship of those who have laid hold of the redemption offered by God through Christ.

Thus, human nature calls for a *community* as the channel of divine activity in redemption, while that activity itself is distinct from the channel through which it operates. It is a vital element in Christian faith that God himself, and not man (any tendency of human nature in general), takes the initiative in redemption, as he does in creation. That community, or channel of redemption, is the Body of Christ and Scripture makes this crystal clear.

St. Paul said:

"(God) put everything in subjection beneath his feet and appointed (Christ) as supreme head to the Church, which is his body . . . " (Eph. i. 23).

"(N)o one ever hated his own body: on the contrary, he provides and cares for it; and that is how Christ treats the church, because it is his body, of which we are the living parts" (Eph. v. 29).

"(Christ) is, moreover, the head of the body, the church. He is its origin, the first to return from the dead, to be in all things alone supreme" (Col. i. 18).

"(I)t is from the Head that the whole body, with all its joints and ligaments, receives its supplies, and thus knit together grows according to God's design" (Col. ii. 19).

"For Christ is like a single body with its many links and organs, which, many as they are, together make up one body. For indeed we were all brought into one body by baptism, in the one Spirit . . .

"Now you are Christ's body, and each of you a link or organ of it" (I Cor. xii. 12, 13, 27).

To sum up the Biblical description of the Church, she is the "bride" of Christ which he is to present to himself "glorious, without spot" (Eph. v. 27) — a description of the Church as destined one day to be perfected (Rev. xxi 9); as the "body" of Christ, of which the faithful are "members" (I Cor. xii 12-27), and of which Christ is the "head" (Eph. i. 22; iv. 15; Col. i. 18); as the sphere within which, it is implied, the Spirit specially operates (Eph. iv. 4): and as being destined to grow up in Christ into unity so as to constitute in him the "fulness" of Christ who is at last to be "all and in all" (Eph. iv. 13; i. 23; Col. iii. 11).

While the Church may be conceived of in many ways ("those called out," the "kingdom of God," the "New Israel"), it is primarily spoken of as the "Body of Christ". Even in the middle of the second century, we see the Church so described. The sub-apostolic *Second Epistle to the Corinthians*, ascribed to St. Clement, but probably written around A.D. 140, states, in chapter 14:

"The Church exists not now for the first time, but has been from the beginning: for she was spiritual, as our Jesus was also spiritual, but was manifested in the last days . . . . The living Church is the body of Christ . . . . Now the Church, being spiritual, was manifested in the flesh of Christ, for this flesh is the counterpart and copy of the spirit."

Hermas, Justin, Clement and other early Fathers used terms of description as "one body," "holy," and "catholic" (e.g. Church of Smyrna, *Martyrdom of Polycarp*, sent to all communities comprising "the holy and Catholic Church"). In all of these statements it is implied that the Church is one, by virtue of the divine life pulsing through it. Called into existence by God, it is no mere man-made organization, but it is, in fact, an organism, the body of Christ, forming a spiritual unity with him as close as his unity with the Father so that Christians can be called his "members."

The whole relationship is very logical when we realize that Christ came into the world to draw man to God. When Christ left at his Ascension, the work of redemption was not anywhere near complete. It was necessary to carry on the work Our Lord had begun. His physical body was no longer present; yet he still needed hands and feet, eyes and ears, and tongues and minds to carry out the Will of God in the world.

In the New Testament a number of things are called Christ's Body:

1. The natural body in which he lived and died.

2. The glorified body of the Resurrection and Ascension.

3. His mystical body, the Church.

4. His Eucharistic body.

In all of these there is something in common — an embodiment of Our Lord and a means through which the life of the Incarnate is made accessible to man. This includes the Sacraments, the Gospel and the Ministry, as well as the continuity of the Church.

As the Nineteenth Article of Religion says:

"The visible Church of Christ is a congregation of faithful men, in which the pure Word of God is preached, and the Sacraments be duly ministered according to Christ's ordinance, in all those things that of necessity are requisite to the same."

Or even more simply, the Catechism of the Prayer Book says:

"The Church is described as the Body of which Jesus Christ is the Head, and of which all baptized people are the members."

The Church is also described as "one, Holy, Catholic and Apostolic" in the Catechism; as "one Body under one Head" in which the spirit "consecrates its members" and it "proclaims the whole Faith to all people to the end of time" continuing "in the teaching and fellowship of the apostles." There is, therefore, a stream of unity flowing from the Holy Trinity through the Incarnation into the Church, as an essential element in the plan of redemption which God has for us.

CHAPTER 3

Scriptural Basis For The Creeds

In the previous chapter, we examined the principal theological developments within the Church which led to or explained the teaching of the Church as defined in the Creeds. We also heard from the Church Fathers and others in regard to those theological developments.

In this chapter we will take a brief look at the historic and biblical development of the Creeds themselves. While the theology is extremely important in understanding the issues, Scripture is essential for the authority of the credal statements in regard to these matters. In this way we can see that the Creeds are the natural result of both Scripture and Tradition. For, as Article XX of the Articles of Religion states:

> "The Church hath ... authority in Controversies of Faith: and yet it is not lawful for the Church to ordain any thing that is contrary to God's Word written, neither may it so expound one place of Scripture, that it be repugnant to another. Wherefore, although the Church be a witness and a keeper of Holy Writ, yet, as it ought not to decree any thing against the same, so besides the same ought it not to enforce any thing to be believed for necessity of Salvation."

The Creeds primarily used in the Church today are the Apostles' Creed and the Nicene Creed (Article VIII, Articles of Religion). To these might be added the Athanasian Creed, which was, in fact, included in the English version of Article VIII, and has been restored to our Prayer Book (p. 864). However, for the purpose of our discussion, we are concerned with the Baptismal Creed, commonly called the Apostles' Creed, and the great universal statement of Christian Faith, the Nicene Creed.

The Apostles' Creed and the Nicene Creed are found in the Prayer Book and are the "statements of our basic beliefs about God," as the Catechism says. Let us look at the texts of those Creeds, as found on pp. 53, 54, 327 and 328 of the Prayer Book:

The Apostles' Creed

I believe in God, the Father almightly, maker of heaven and earth;

And in Jesus Christ his only Son our Lord; who was conceived by the Holy Ghost, born of the Virgin Mary, suffered under Pontius Pilate, was crucified, dead and buried. He descended into hell. The third day he rose again from the dead. He ascended into heaven, and sitteth on the right hand of God the Father almighty. From thence he shall come to judge the quick and the dead.

I believe in the Holy Ghost, the holy catholic Church, the communion of saints, the forgiveness of sins, the resurrection of the body, and the life everlasting. Amen.

The Nicene Creed

I believe in one God, the Father Almighty, maker of heaven and earth, and of all things visible and invisible;

And in one Lord Jesus Christ, the only-begotten Son of God, begotten of his Father before all worlds, God of God, Light of Light, very God of very God, begotten, not made, being of one substance with the Father; by whom all things were made; who for us men and for our salvation came down from heaven, and was incarnate by the Holy Ghost of the Virgin Mary, and was made man; and was crucified also for us under Pontius Pilate; he suffered and was buried; and the third day he rose again according to the Scriptures, and ascended into heaven, and sitteth on the right hand of the Father; and he shall come again, with glory, to judge both the quick and the dead; whose kingdom shall have no end.

And I believe in the Holy Ghost the Lord, and Giver of Life, who proceedeth from the Father and the Son; who with the Father and the Son together is worshipped and glorified; who spake by the Prophets. And I believe one holy Catholic and Apostolic Church; I acknowledge one Baptism for the remission of sins; and I look for the resurrection of the dead, and the life of the world to come. Amen.

These creeds are not found in Holy Scripture. Indeed, until quite recently it had been the prevailing opinion among theologians that fixed creeds did not come into general use at all in the Church until after New Testament times. However, the beginnings of credal statements may be found in the New Testament and we shall see that the Articles of Faith as contained in the Catholic creeds are, in fact, Scriptural in origin.

From the first, the Church required from all who wished to become members a public profession of faith in Christ. St. Timothy, probably at the moment of his Baptism, had confessed his faith in Christ before many witnesses (I Tim. vi. 12). So, too, in the Baptism of the eunuch by St. Philip, several versions of the Acts of the Apostles contain the following language:

> "As they were going along the road, they came to some water. 'Look,' said the eunuch, 'here is water: what is there to prevent my being baptized?'; Philip said, 'If you wholeheartedly believe, it is permitted.' He replied, 'I believe that Jesus Christ is the Son of God' (Acts viii. 36-37)"

The use of some simple formula is implied in the passages of St. Paul. "No man can say that Jesus is Lord save in the Holy Ghost (I Cor. xii. 3)." "If thou shalt confess with thy mouth Jesus as Lord and shalt believe in thine heart that God has raised him from the dead, thou shalt be saved. For with the heart man believeth unto righteousness and with the mouth confession is made unto salvation (Rom. x. 9-10)." The same is also suggested by St. John. "Whosoever shall confess that Jesus is the Son of God, God abides in him and he in God (I Jn. iv. 15)." So too, in the fifth chapter, verse 5, the context points to a connection between the confession that "Jesus is the Son of God" and the coming by water, i.e. Baptism. The language suggests a form of baptismal confession, "I believe that Jesus is the Son of God."

When we tie these brief baptismal confessions of faith to the formula for Baptism given by Our Lord, "Baptize men everywhere in the name of the Father and the Son and the Holy Spirit, and teach them to observe all that I have commanded you (Matt. xxviii. 19)," we already have a New Testament beginning of a simple baptismal statement of belief, a creed. In fact the old Roman baptismal symbol, the germ of the Apostles' Creed, written before the end of the first century while parts of the New Testament had not yet been written, provides us with the beginning of a baptismal creed rooted in the New Testament.

St. Paul, writing about A.D. 55, in his first Epistle to the Corinthians, gives us at least five articles of a primitive formula of faith or creed. The five articles, almost certainly quoted from an earlier source by St. Paul, are these:

1. Christ died for our sins according to the Scriptures.

2. He was buried.

3. He has been raised on the third day according to the Scriptures.

4. He appeared to Cephas.

5. Then to the twelve.

"And now my brothers, I must remind you of the gospel that I preached to you; the gospel which you received, on which you have taken your stand, and which is now bringing you salvation. Do you remember the terms in which I preached the gospel to you? — For I assume you did not accept it thoughtlessly.

"First and foremost, I handed on to you the facts which had been imparted to me: That Christ died for our sins, in accordance with the Scriptures; that he was buried; that he was raised to life on the third day, according to the Scriptures; that he appeared to Cephas, and afterwards to the twelve (I Cor. xv. 1-5)."

Based upon these early credal statements and the universal custom of Baptism with instruction, Charles Harris, writing in "A New Commentary on Holy Scripture," states that there had arisen at Jerusalem, as early as A.D. 35, a seven article statement of faith, including the five articles above quoted from St. Paul, and, in addition, the following:

6. He is seated at the right hand of God.

7. He shall come again to judge the quick and the dead.

To these seven articles may be added the general declaration "Jesus Christ is Lord."

If this be true, then even before a single word of the New Testament was written, the primitive Church at Jerusalem was using a baptismal creed somewhat along the following form:

> "I believe that Jesus Christ is Lord; that he died for our sins, was buried, and raised on the third day according to the Scriptures; that he appeared to Cephas and the twelve; that he is seated at the right hand of God and shall come again to judge the quick and the dead."

If we add to that the Trinitarian formula of Baptism, we can see quite readily the outline of the Apostles' Creed.

While the theory put forth by Harris may be just that, a theory, and while it may never be subject to clear and irrefutable proof, it does show the justification for study of credal statements in Holy Scripture. As a matter of history, the Apostles' Creed as we know it today is a development and expansion of an earlier Roman Baptismal Creed, the roots of which date back to the latter part of the first century.

The Nicene Creed is an expansion of the Apostles' Creed by including a number of definitive statements concerning the divinity of Our Lord, together with a brief explication of the operation of the Holy Spirit.

The Apostles' Creed has authority in the Church because of its antiquity, with roots reaching into the Apostolic age. The Nicene Creed, on the other hand, was first promulgated by the Council of Nicaea in A.D. 325, and then expanded by the Council of Constantinople in A.D. 381 to the present form in which we now have it. Its authority is therefore a result of a consensus by the whole Church in Council assembled. We will therefore examine the Scriptural bases of the Articles of the Apostles' Creed in its present form, together with Scriptural references to the expanded form of the Nicene Creed.

The Apostles' Creed begins with an affirmation of faith, "I believe in God, the Father almighty." Against this we see Scriptural statements such as "God is our Father, and God alone" (Jn. viii. 41); "For us there is one God, the Father" (I

Cor. viii. 6). We then affirm that God is "maker of heaven and earth", words reflecting the beginning of creation "When God made Heaven and Earth" (Gen. i. 1) and the words of St. John "All things were made by him; and without him was not anything made that was made" (Jn. i. 3).

To this opening paragraph of the Apostles' Creed, the Nicene Creed adds the words "and of all things visible and invisible." This clause is a reflection of Paul's language in the first chapter of his Epistle to the Colossians, when he speaks of Christ being the image of the Father: "In him everything in heaven and on earth was created, not only things visible but also the invisible orders of thrones, sovereignties, authorities and powers."

The second paragraph of the Creed opens with an affirmation of our belief in Jesus Christ as God's "only Son Our Lord." The Nicene Creed uses the expression "the only begotten Son of God." These phrases, "the only Son," and "the only begotten Son," are found throughout the New Testament, as in John iii. 16, 18; Heb. xi. 17; I Jn. iv. 9. The Nicene Creed goes on to add further declaratory statements concerning Our Lord:

> "begotten of his Father before all worlds, God of God, Light of Light, very God of very God."

The language is reminiscent of the first chapter of the Gospel according to St. John:

> "When all things began, the Word already was. The Word dwelt with God, and what God was, the Word was. The Word, then, was with God at the beginning, and through him all things came to be; no single thing was created without him. All that came to be was alive with his life, and that life was the light of men. The light shines on in the dark, and the darkness has never mastered it.

> "There appeared a man named John, sent from God; He came as a witness to testify to the light, that all might become believers through him. He was not himself the light; he came to bear witness to the light. The real light which enlightens ever man was even then coming into the world .... So the word became flesh; he came to dwell among us and we saw his glory, such glory as befits the Father's only son, full of grace and truth" (Jn. i. 1-18).

The Nicene Creed goes on to tell us that Jesus Christ is "of one substance with the Father" and that "all things were made" by him. In this, the creeds echo the statement of Our Lord, "My Father and I are one" (Jn. x. 30), and Paul's statement concerning Christ, "The whole universe has been created through him" (Col. i. 17), as well as the statement of John, "Through him (the Word made flesh) all things came to be; no single thing was created without him" (Jn. i. 3).

The Apostles' Creed goes on to assert that Our Lord was "conceived by the Holy Ghost", and "born of the Virgin Mary." Matthew states, "(Mary) found that she was with child by the Holy Spirit" (Matt. i. 18). When Joseph desired to have the marriage contract set aside, an Angel of the Lord appeared to him and said, "Do not be afraid to take Mary home with you as your wife. It is by the Holy Spirit that she has conceived this child. She will bear a son; and you shall give him the name Jesus (Saviour), for he will save his people from their sins" (Matt. i. 20, 21). Or, as St. John said in the opening of his Gospel, "The Word was made flesh and dwelled among us."

St. Luke records for us that when the angel first told Mary that she was to be the mother of God's Son, she questioned, "How can this be? I am still a virgin." The angel answered, "The Holy Spirit will come upon you, and the power of the Most High will overshadow you; and for that reason the holy child to be born will be called 'Son of God'" (Lk. i. 34, 35).

The Apostles' Creed then contains four extremely important words, "suffered under Pontius Pilate." This tells us that Our Lord was truly human and was capable of suffering. It also tells us that he lived in the first half of the first century in the Roman province of Judea, during the rule of Pontius Pilate as Roman Governor. Our Lord himself tells us that he was to suffer under Pontius Pilate, for as he said to the disciples on the way to Emmaus, "Was the Messiah not bound to suffer thus before entering upon his glory?" (Lk. xxiv. 26). Paul also taught the same thing, as Luke records; "Paul went to their meeting; and for the next three sabaths he argued with them, quoting texts of Scripture which he expounded and applied to show that the messiah had to suffer and rise from the dead" (Acts xvii. 2, 3). It was Pilate who directed that he be crucified, as the Nicene Creed specifically states. As Scripture says, "Then at last, to satisfy them, Pilate handed Jesus over to be crucified" (Jn. xix. 16). The Creeds also assert that Christ actually died and was buried. This is simply a reflection of the early credal form cited by St. Paul:

> "First and foremost, I handed on to you the facts which had been imparted to me: That Christ died for our sins, in accordance with the Scriptures; that he was buried . . ." (I Cor. xv. 3).

In the Apostles' Creed, there then appears a phrase missing from the Nicene Creed, "He descended into hell." Does this word *hell* mean that Jesus suffered some kind of damnation, or did he go some place other than the place of everlasting damnation? The word *hell*, as used in the Apostles' Creed, refers to the abode of the dead (an intermediate state) rather than a place of everlasting punishment. The confusion is due to the fact that the original text was in Greek, and the Greek word was *hades*. *Hades* expresses two entirely different concepts, both of which are found in the Hebrew Scripture. One of these concepts is a place of departed spirits, *sheol*. The second is *gehenna*, a place of everlasting punishment and damnation. Both *sheol* and *gehenna* are translated into Greek as *hades*. The word *hades* is translated into English as *hell*. For most English speaking people, *hell* means a place of punishment, not the intermediate abode of the spirits of the dead. Thus the confusion over the phrase, "He descended into hell."

In order to end this confusion, the rubric in the 1928 Prayer Book states "and any Churches may, instead of the words, *He descended into Hell*, use the words, *He went to the place of departed spirits*, which are considered as words of the same meaning in the Creed." The 1979 Prayer Book dealt with the matter by providing an alternative translation of the Apostles' Creed, in which the phrase reads "He descended to the dead."

Scripture makes it quite clear that Jesus' spirit went to the place of departed spirits, or the intermediate abode of the dead, not to the place of punishment. St. Peter records this fact for us in his first Epistle General:

> "In the body he was put to death; in the spirit he was brought to life. And in the spirit he went and made his proclamation to the imprisoned spirits. . . . Why was the gospel preached to those who are dead? In order that,

although in the body they received the sentence common to men, they might in the spirit be alive with the life of God" (I Pet. iii. 19; iv. 6).

The Apostles' Creed then goes on to assert that "The third day he rose again from the dead." The Nicene Creed states "And the third day he rose again according to the Scriptures." This language is almost identical to that used by St. Paul who stated that "He was raised to life on the third day, according to the Scriptures" (I. Cor. xv. 4). Scriptures are replete with references to Our Lord's resurrection (Mk. xvi. 6; Matt. xxviii. 6; Lk. xxiv. 7; Jn. xx. 9; Acts i. 22; I Cor. xv. 13; I Pet. i. 3).

As Scripture records his resurrection, it also records that he ascended into heaven, as both Creeds assert. The account of Our Lord's Ascension is recorded in the first chapter of the Acts of the Apostles (Acts i. 9-11), which also records that he will return even as he has ascended. St. Luke also refers to this in his Gospel (Lk. xxiv. 51): "And in the act of blessing he parted from them and was carried up into heaven." St. Paul also asserts the ascension of Our Lord (Ephes. iv. 8-10). Our Lord himself said that he would ascend to heaven, "But go to my brothers and tell them I am going to ascend to my Father and your Father, my God and your God" (Jn. xx. 17).

The Creeds assert that Our Lord has the highest place of honor, that is, he is seated at "the right hand of God the Father almighty". St. Paul tells us, "Aspire to the realms above, where Christ is, seated at the right hand of God" (Col. iii. 1). Again, Paul says that God raised Jesus "from the dead, when he enthroned him at his right hand in the heavenly realms" (Ephes. i. 21). Our Lord prophesied this when he said at his own trial, "You will see the Son of Man seated at the right hand of God and coming with the clouds of heaven" (Mk. xiv. 62). Mark also records that Our Lord was seated at the right hand of God after his ascension: "So after talking with them the Lord Jesus was taken up into heaven, and he took his seat at the right hand of God" (Mk. xvi. 19).

The Creeds next assert that Christ shall return to judge the living and the dead. St. Paul cites this over and over again, as for example when he wrote St. Timothy, "Before God, and before Christ Jesus who is to judge men, living and dead, I charge you solemnly by his coming appearance and his reign, proclaim the message" (II Tim. iv. 1, 2). He also reminds the

Church at Thessalonika of the judgment of the living and dead (I Thes. v.). Our Lord himself gives us a picture of the final judgment in Matthew's Gospel:

> "When the Son of Man comes in his glory and all the angels with him, he will sit in state on his throne, with all the nations gathered before him. He will separate men into two groups, as a shepherd separates the sheep from the goats" (Matt. xxv. 31, 32).

The judgment of Our Lord will come at the end of this world, according to St. John:

> "Then I saw a great white throne, and the One who sat upon it; from His presence earth and heaven vanished away, and no place was left for them. I could see the dead, great and small, standing before the throne; and books were opened. Then another book was opened, and the roll of the living. From what was written in these books the dead were judged upon the record of their deeds" (Rev. xx. 11, 12).

The final paragraph of each Creed begins with a statement of belief in the Holy Spirit. However, the Nicene Creed expands this by stating that the Spirit is "the Lord, and Giver of Life," and proceeds "from the Father and (or through) the Son; who with the Father and the Son together is worshiped and glorified; who spake by the Prophets." It was the Holy Spirit through Whose power Jesus Christ was born (Lk. i. 35; Matt. i. 20). It is the Holy Spirit who descends upon Our Lord at his Baptism in the form of a dove (Mk. i. 9, 10) and the Holy Spirit is Lord against whom we may not blaspheme (Mk. iii. 29). John records Our Lord's words concerning the Holy Spirit:

> "When your Advocate has come, whom I will send you from the Father — the Spirit of truth that issues from the Father — he will bear witness to me" (Jn. xv. 26).

The Holy Spirit guides into truth, so that one may prophesy or speak through the guidance of the Spirit. "However, when he comes who is the spirit of truth, he will guide you into all the truth; for he will not speak on his own authority, but will tell only what he hears" (Jn. xvi. 12, 13).

Next the Creeds speak of the Church, and refer specifically to the four marks of the Church as being One, Holy, Catholic and Apostolic. We are told that the Church is the Body of Christ, and that there is but one body (I Cor. xii. 13). Unity is a necessary part of the Church, for as St. Paul says, "There is one body and one spirit, as there is also one hope held out in God's call to you; one Lord, one faith, one baptism; one God and Father of all" (Ephes. iv. 4-6).

The Church is called Holy because it is separated or set apart for the service of God, and is the means of the glory of the eternal future which is God's promise to all his sanctified people (I Pet. i. 15; Ephes. i. 18). The final holiness of the Church is portrayed for us in Revelations xxi. 9 to xxii. 5 in the image of the Holy City Jerusalem into which are gathered all the people of God and from which the glory of God's presence excludes all that is unclean.

The Church is Catholic, that is, universal. The Catechism defines this as holding the whole faith for all time, in all countries, and for all people. In Scripture we see that the Church is for all people, and in Christ, distinctions of race and position are abolished (Gal. iii. 28; Col. iii. 10, 11). The Church is sent to the whole world to baptize all people and make all nations disciples of Our Lord (Matt. xxviii. 19).

Finally, the Church is described as Apostolic because it follows steadfastly in the Apostles' teaching and fellowship (Acts ii. 42). The Church is built upon the foundation of the Apostles (Ephes. ii. 19, 20; Matt. xvi. 18; Rev. xxi. 14).

The Nicene Creed speaks of belief in one Baptism for the remission of sins. St. Paul speaks of one Baptism (Ephes. iv. 5) and Baptism is the means by which we receive forgiveness of sins (Acts ii. 38; Acts xxii. 16).

The Apostles' Creed speaks of the Communion of Saints, a belief in the unity of the Church for both the living and the dead, for all people in all times (Ephes. ii. 19; iv. 4-6). Finally, St. Paul reminds us that the Church is the Body of Christ of which all faithful persons are members (I Cor. xii. 12-27).

The final phrases of both Creeds state a belief in the Resurrection of the Body and the Life Everlasting. Our Lord promised eternal life to those who followed him and who kept his eucharistic command. "Whoever eats my flesh and drinks my blood possesses eternal life and I will raise him up on the last day" (Jn. vi. 54). St. Paul has two very important passages on this subject, the first of these being the most famous passage (I Cor. xv. 12-57). In this passage Paul tells us that Christ is the first fruits of all who sleep in death, that resurrection of the body is a fact and that in the resurrection we become imperishable and incorruptible, possessing an immortality, leading to the ultimate conquest of death. He reiterates the same idea in another Epistle (I Thes. iv. 13-18). Paul states that we should not grieve like other men who have no hope, for we believe that "Jesus died and rose again; and so it will be for those who die as Christians; God will bring them to life with Jesus."

So now we can see the beginning of development of credal statements in the New Testament, the formulating of Articles of Faith, the relationship of those Articles of Faith to Christian Baptism, and the natural development of the Baptismal Creed, which becomes the Apostles' Creed, and becomes the basis for the expanded Nicene Creed. Finally, we see that all of the Articles of Faith as contained in the Creeds are Scriptural in their bases. Therefore, we could say with Charles Harris, that even though the Trinitarian Creed may not be found intact in Holy Scripture, "Nevertheless, all the materials needed for constructing it are already present."

PART III

The Sacraments

Article XXV of the Articles of Religion states:

"Sacraments ordained of Christ be not only badges or tokens of Christian men's profession, but rather they be certain sure witnesses, and the effectual signs of grace, and God's good will towards us, by the which he doth work invisibly in us, and doth not only quicken, but also strengthen and confirm our Faith in him."

Chapter 4 deals with the Sacrament(s) of Christian Initiation, that is, Baptism and Confirmation. Chapter 5 deals with the Eucharist, and Chapter 6 with three of the other four "commonly called Sacraments," Penance, Holy Matrimony and Holy Unction. Holy Orders is dealt with in part IV, as this Sacrament is one of the main points of the Quadrilateral.

While we often speak of "the Seven Sacraments," it should be noted that the word "sacrament" does not appear anywhere in the New Testament, nor does Scripture outline a detailed or developed sacramental system. Article XXV, cited above, goes on to say:

"There are two Sacraments ordained of Christ Our Lord in the Gospel, that is to say, Baptism, and the Supper of the Lord.

"Those five commonly called Sacraments, that is to say, Confirmation, Penance, Orders, Matrimony, and Extreme Unction, are not to be counted for Sacraments of the Gospel, being such as have grown partly of the corrupt following of the Apostles, partly are states of life allowed in the Scriptures; but yet have not like nature of Sacraments with Baptism, and the Lord's Supper, for that they have not any visible sign or ceremony ordained of God."

Similarly, in *The Book of Common Prayer* we read in the Catechism about the Sacraments of Holy Baptism and the Holy Eucharist, then read the following:

"Q. What other sacramental rites evolved in the Church under the guidance of the Holy Spirit?

"A. Other sacramental rites which evolved in the Church include confirmation, ordination, holy matrimony, reconciliation of penitent, and unction.

"Q. How do they differ from the two Sacraments of the Gospel?

"A. Although they are means of grace, they are not necessary for all persons in the same way that Baptism and the Eucharist are.

* * *

"Q. Is God's activity limited to these rites?

"A. God does not limit Himself to these rites; they are patterns of countless ways by which God uses material things to reach out to us."

The Catholic Church has for many centuries spoken of the "Seven Sacraments" but this numerology is not found in Holy Scripture. In the Prayer Book a Sacrament is defined as an outward and visible sign of an inward and spiritual grace ordained of Christ. In the strict sense of the word Holy Scripture only describes two sacraments, the Sacrament of Christian Initiation and the Sacrament of the Eucharist. (Christian Initiation would appear to embrace both Baptism and Confirmation.) As to the others, there is no "outward and visible sign of an inward and spiritual grace, the form of which is ordained by Christ himself."

In the writing of the Early Church Fathers, St. John Chrysostom uses the Greek term *mysterion*, or *sacrament* to apply to both Christ's humiliation and crucifixion and to Holy Baptism. Hilary uses the Latin term *sacramentum* to apply not only to the Eucharist and Baptism but also to the mystery of the Divine Unity, or of the Lord's Divinity, or of the Incarnation.

For Cyril of Jerusalem and Ambrose there were three sacraments — Baptism, Confirmation or Chrism, and the Eucharist. The language of Gregory of Nyssa about Ordination and of Chrysostom about Penance suggest that these, too, qualified for the title of "Sacrament" in their eyes.

Augustine illustrates both the wider and narrower meaning of *sacramentum*. "Signs are called sacraments," he explains, "when they have reference to divine things." On this definition anything might be a sacrament which is a token, natural or conventional, of a divine reality. Thus, he can include under the term such rites as the blessed salt handed to catechumens, the baptismal exorcisms, and the formal tradition of the Creed and the Lord's Prayer to catechumens as well as the Old Testament events and personages mysteriously foreshadowing Christ and his salvation. However, on the other hand, he speaks of Baptism and the Eucharist as being specific instances of *sacramentum*.

It is only gradually over the centuries that the Catholic Church has developed the concept of Seven Sacraments and the Anglican Communion has never bound itself rigorously to the concept that there are no less or more than seven rites entitled to the name "sacrament." Therefore, in the following chapters we will examine Christian Initiation and the Eucharist in detail, from the perspectives of the Church's teaching and Scripture. For the remaining rites, we will only touch on them from the Scriptural point of view. (It should be noted, as mentioned above, that part IV discusses Holy Orders in detail as the final essential of the Faith.)

CHAPTER 4

Christian Initiation

In commissioning his Apostles Our Lord said, "Go forth therefore and make all nations my disciples; baptize men everywhere in the name of the Father and the Son and the Holy Spirit" (Matt. xxviii. 19). Our Lord had taught that Baptism was to be the necessary condition of entrance into the Kingdom of God and an instrument of new birth of the Spirit. "In truth I tell you, no one can enter the kingdom of God without being born from water and spirit" (Jn. iii. 5).

If we must be born of water and the Spirit in order to enter the kingdom of Heaven, what is involved in this New Birth? And why has Our Lord chosen Baptism as the means of grace? Jesus utilized common, everyday things as the vehicles for the giving of God's grace. Since a physical washing is the normal means of cleaning physical things which are dirty (hands, dishes, clothes), then a spiritual washing would be the means of cleansing a soul that is spiritually dirty, or sin-stained. A ceremonial washing or baptism was common in the religions of antiquity, where it generally symbolized a spiritual cleansing. Among the Jews, for example, a ceremonial washing was the first step for proselytes from the Gentile world. This baptism cleansed them from the stains of heathenism and made them fit to be joined with the chosen people of God.

This ritual cleansing was practiced in Our Lord's day. In fact, he chose to submit to this cleansing at the beginning of his ministry when he received baptism at the hands of his cousin, John the Baptist. The baptism of Jesus became for the Church the basis and example of its own rite of initiation. However, the ritual baptism of spiritual cleansing, even by John the Baptist, was not the same thing as the Christian sacrament of Baptism. In the first place, John's baptism was simply a sign of repentance, not a Sacrament of New Birth:

"I baptize you with water, for repentance; but the one who comes after me is mightier than I . . . He will baptize you with the Holy Spirit and with fire" (Matt. iii. 11).

Secondly, Christian Initiation involved *both* water (baptism) and the reception of the Holy Spirit (confirmation). Thus, those baptized only by a ceremonial washing as a sign of repentance were required to receive a *Christian* baptism and the confirmation or sealing of the Spirit. This is because Jewish baptism and even John's baptism was *only* with water while the Christian Initiation that admits into the Kingdom of God is "of water and Spirit." Thus we are told:

"While Apollos was at Corinth, Paul travelled through the inland regions till he came to Ephesus. There he found a number of converts, to whom he said, 'Did you receive the Holy Spirit when you became believers?' 'No,' they replied, 'We have not even heard that there is a Holy Spirit.' He said, 'Then what baptism were you given?' 'John's baptism,' they answered. Paul then said, 'The baptism that John gave was a baptism in token of repentance, and he told the people to put their trust in one who was to come after him, that is, in Jesus.' On hearing this they were baptized into the name of the Lord Jesus; and when Paul had laid his hands on them, the Holy Spirit came upon them . . . " (Acts xix. 1-6).

Water and Spirit — these two are intimately associated with Christian Initiation. Paul's custom was to baptize (with water) and lay hands on the converts and they received the Holy Spirit. Generally, Christian Initiation involved this twofold action; washing with water and reception of the Spirit by the laying on of hands. Thus Christians were regenerated (born anew) by water and Spirit as Our Lord had told Nicodemus. A form of this is seen in Our Lord's baptism where he comes up out of the *water* and the *Spirit*, in the form of a dove, descends upon him (Mark i. 10-11). This union of baptism and the Holy Spirit is referred to time and time again in Scripture:

"He (Jesus) saved us through the water of rebirth and the renewing power of the Holy Spirit" (Tit. iii. 5).

"Repent and be baptized, every one of you, in the name of Jesus the Messiah for the forgiveness of your sins; and you will receive the gift of the Holy Spirit" (Acts ii. 38).

CHRISTIAN INITIATION

The Christian Initiation normally involved both washing (baptism) and laying on of hands (confirmation). The laying on of hands was associated with the completion of the initiatory rite and the bestowal of the Holy Spirit (Acts xix.). Sometimes this completion of rite was referred to as being "sealed" in the Lord (II Cor. i. 22; Ephes. i. 13).

The laying on of hands or seal of the reception of the Spirit, which we call Confirmation, usually accompanied the Baptism (e.g. Acts xix. 6) but sometimes was separated from it in time:

> "The Apostles in Jerusalem now heard that Samaria had accepted the word of God. They sent off Peter and John, who went down there and prayed for the converts, asking that they might receive the Holy Spirit. For until then the Spirit had not come upon any of them. They had been baptized into the name of the Lord Jesus, that and nothing more. So Peter and John laid their hands on them and they received the Holy Spirit" (Acts viii. 14-17).

This laying on of hands is counted, along with baptism, as a foundation belonging to the first principals of the Christian system (Heb. vi. 1, 2). St. Peter taught that the gift of the Holy Spirit was the immediate sequel of baptism (Acts ii. 38) and in apostolic teaching and practice confirmation was held to be the means of receiving this gift. Consequently the Apostles habitually administered confirmation by laying on of hands as soon as practicable after baptism (Acts viii. 17-18; xix 6). Thus the New Testament shows that confirmation is the proper and normal complement of baptism. At the same time the Apostles clearly distinguished between the two rites, both in time and in their benefits (Acts viii. 15-17).

What, then, are the benefits of baptism? The New Testament tells us:

(1) Baptism remits sins:

> "(B)e baptized . . . for the forgiveness of your sins" (Acts ii. 38).

> "Be baptized . . . and wash away your sins" (Acts xxii. 16).

(2) Through baptism, we share in Christ's death, and thus his resurrection:

"... When we were baptized into union with Christ Jesus we were baptized into his death (.) By baptism we were buried with him, and lay dead, in order that, as Christ was raised from the dead ... so also we ..." (Rom. vi. 4).

"For in baptism you were buried with him, in baptism also you were raised to life with him through your faith in the active power of God who raised him from the dead" (Col. ii. 12).

(3) By baptism, we are made the children of God:

"For through faith you are all sons of God in union with Christ Jesus. Baptized into union with him, you have all put on Christ ... To prove that you are sons, God has sent into our hearts the Spirit of his Son, crying 'Abba! Father!' You are ... by God's own act an heir" (Gal. iii. 26, 27; iv. 6, 7).

(4) By baptism, we are made a part of the Body of Christ.

"For indeed we were all brought into one body by baptism ... Now you are Christ's body, and each of you a limb or organ of it" (l Cor. xxii. 13, 27).

(5) Baptism takes the place in the New Covenant which was occupied by circumcision in the Old:

"In him also you were circumcised, not in a physical sense ... (baptism) is Christ's way of circumcision" (Col. ii. 11).

(6) Baptism gives us salvation from sin:

"Baptism ... brings salvation" (l Pet. iii. 21).

"Jesus saved us through the water of rebirth" (Tit. iii. 5).

What are the benefits of confirmation? Through confirmation we receive the Holy Spirit:

"So Peter and John laid their hands on them and they received the Holy Spirit" (Acts vii. 17).

"(W)hen Paul had laid this hands on them, the Holy Spirit came upon them ... " (Acts xix. 7).

Moreover, following Our Lord's baptism, he received the Holy Spirit in the form of a dove (Matt. iii. 16). This outpouring of the Spirit was a formal bestowal of gifts upon Christ, in other words, his anointing. In several passages of the Apocalypse, Our Lord is represented as having the Seven Spirits of God, a distributive personification of his spiritual equipment (Rev. i. 4; iv. 5; v. 6). In the prophecy of Isaiah it was said of the Messiah:

"The spirit of the Lord shall rest upon him, a spirit of wisdom and understanding, a spirit of counsel and power, a spirit of knowledge and true godliness, and the fear of the Lord" (Isa. xi. 2;) (Septuagint).

Therefore, as the descent of the Holy Spirit upon Our Lord is a type of our own reception of the Spirit in confirmation, we say that we receive the Seven Gifts of the Spirit, as Our Lord did, at our own confirmation.

To reiterate: Christian Initiation (baptism and confirmation) remits sins, opens the door to everlasting life, makes us children of God, grafts us into Christ, saves us, and gives us the strengthening gifts of the Spirit. Or, to put it into Scriptual language, in baptism the grace of God is given for regeneration, remission, justification and sanctification. In confirmation the gifts of the Spirit are given for equipment and strength in the journey Godward.

How, then, can we sin after being born again of water and the Spirit? Regeneration, conveyed by baptism, is a seed of promise. As a seed, the growth of a life in Christ is only potential, not actual. As a factor in salvation, regeneration is closely associated with conversion and the conduct of a converted Christian is the proper fruit of regeneration. However, regeneration is not the same thing as conversion, even as the seed is not the same thing as the fruit. St. John clearly distinguishes between the seed (regeneration) and the freedom from sin (conversion) which may spring from it (I John iii. 9, 10: I John i. 8-10).

St. Paul also points out that it is possible to sin (fall from grace) after baptism. He rebukes the Corinthian Christians, who are reminded that their gifts of grace may be received in vain (2 Cor. vi. 1). He also warns the Church of Galatia that Christians can fall from grace (Gal. v. 4). (However, if we do fall from grace, our sins after baptism may be forgiven

(James v. 15; I John i. 9).) We must "grow in grace." The seed of promise must be nurtured to fruition. This means we have to strive for the use of the gifts of grace imparted to us by the operation of the Spirit. In other words, we are told: "You must work out your own salvation in fear and trembling" (Phil. ii. 12).

While God does pour his Grace and Spirit out upon us in the Sacrament, nonetheless, we must respond to that grace and cooperate with it. If this response is interrupted by our sin, the benefits of the Sacrament are suspended. Baptism is a "sacrament of responsibility." Many of St. Paul's admonitions to sinful Christians bear witness to their having fallen from grace; and the fact they once had grace, and that it is restored after repentance, is clearly implied (Acts viii. 13, 18-23; I Cor. iii. 16, 17; v. 3-5; vi. 11-20; ix. 26, 27; Gal. v. 2, 4, 19-21).

Baptismal character is an indelible seal or spiritual mark, which evermore differentiates the regenerate from the unregenerate (2 Cor. i. 21, 22; Ephes. i. 13, 14; iv. 30; Rev. ix. 4). Because of this, baptism should not be repeated. Like our natural birth, it is a "once in a lifetime" event.

If, then, baptism is an indelible seal, and the means of our salvation, who needs baptism? The answer to this question is, "everybody." As Our Lord said, "Baptize men everywhere." Again, as he said to Nicodemus, "No one can enter the Kingdom of God without being born of water and the Spirit." This requirement includes children. Our Lord said, "Let the children come to me; do not try to stop them; for the Kingdom of God belongs to such as these" (Mark x. 14). Further, children were part of a first century household and the whole household, that is, *all* of its members, would be baptized in the New Testament Church. "(Lydia was baptized, and her household with her" (Acts xvi. 15). "Then they spoke the word of the Lord to him and to everyone in his house . . . and immediately afterwards, (the jailer) and his whole family were baptized" (Acts xvi. 32, 33). Finally, St. Paul wrote to children, as Christians" "Children, obey your parents in everything, for that is pleasing to God and is the Christian way" (Col. iii. 20). Paul repeats this admonition in his letter to the Christians at Ephesus (Ephes. vi. 1).

Early Christian thinking followed Jewish thinking in regarding a household as a unity. When the head of the household became a Christian it was inconceivable that all the members of the household would not enter the new life in Christ together, including servants and children.

What words denote baptism? Our Lord says that we must baptize everywhere "in the name of the Father and the Son and the Holy Spirit." However, several passages indicate that Baptism was in "the name of the Lord Jesus" (Acts ii. 38; viii. 16). On the other hand, St. Paul speaks of being "baptized unto Moses" (I Cor. x. 2), with an implied contrast to being "baptized into Christ." This, of course, does not mean that the formula "unto Moses" was ever used. Further, the *Didache* uses both forms. Apparently the phrase "baptized in the name of Lord Jesus" was used simply as an abbreviation by the writer for the full formula. For example, Eusebius of Caesarea quotes the text of Matt. xxviii. 19; sometimes he cites the full formula and sometimes he abbreviates the formula to "baptizing them in the name of the Lord." At the very best, any formula but baptism in the name of the Trinity is questionable and there is no solid evidence that any other formula was ever used. (Nicholas I of Rome appears to have recognized baptism "in the name of Jesus Christ" as valid, but his opinion is not accepted by any part of the Church. See C. B. Moss, *The Christian Faith.*)

What must be used for the baptism? Our Lord says that we must be "born from *water* and Spirit." All instances given in the New Testament refer to "water" and no other substance (e.g. Tit. iii. 5; Acts viii. 36; Acts x. 47). Moreover, the New Testament Greek word *"baptizein"* means to wash and washing implies water. (The Latin word "lavare", meaning "to wash," is the root for our word "lavatory.")

The method of baptism is either by dipping (immersion) or pouring (affusion). Both methods of washing were and are used. For example, in the ancient world if you wash (baptize) your hands you would either fill the basin with water and dip your hands in the water (immersion) or you would pour the water over your hands from the pitcher (affusion). In today's world you might take a tub bath (immersion) or a shower bath (affusion). While the New Testament does not spell this out, St. Paul baptized a jailer and his whole family in a prison (Acts xvi. 33) where there would not be sufficient water for immersion and affusion would have been the method. On the other hand, there is no indication that immersion was *not* used, as for example, when the eunuch and Philip "went down into the water" (Acts viii. 38).

Who may baptize? Baptism was apparently not limited to the Apostles; St. Philip the Deacon baptized the eunuch as he had earlier baptized the Samaritans (Acts viii. 12). Further, St. Paul was apparently baptized by a lay disciple, Ananias (Acts ix. 19). Finally, Baptism is to the New Covenant what circumcision was to the Old Convenant (Col. ii. 11). Circumcision could be administered by anyone, and by analogy, so can baptism.

Having reviewed the nature and meaning of baptism, we now take a look at confirmation.

Just as baptism is for all people, so is confirmation. In those instances when baptism was administered without the laying on of hands (e.g. St. Philip the Deacon, Acts viii. 12), the sealing of confirmation was later added by the apostles (Acts viii. 17). The author of Hebrews tells us that confirmation is a Christian foundation equal to baptism (Heb. vi. 2).

Unlike baptism, Our Lord gave us no set words for confirmation, just as he gave us no set form for confirmation. Laying on of hands was often used, as we saw above (Acts viii. 17; Acts xix. 6; Heb. vi. 2). Anointing with oil was also apparently used. St. Paul wrote to the Corinthian Christians, "(W)e belong to Christ, guaranteed as his and anointed" (2 Cor. i. 21). St. John speaks even more clearly:

> "You, no less than they, are among those who have an anointing" (I John ii. 20).

> "But as for you, the anointing which you received from (Christ) stays with you" (I John ii. 27).

Further, the reception of the Holy Spirit in confirmation is compared to the descent of the Spirit upon Our Lord at his baptism, often referred to as his "anointing." (Acts x. 38.) Even the title "Christ" given to Our Lord and the name "Christian" given to us comes from the word for anointing, "chrism."

Confirmation, whether by laying on of hands or by anointing was always administered by an Apostle. There is no example given of an Elder, Deacon or Layman doing so. In fact, when Philip the Deacon baptized the Samaritans (Acts viii. 12), the Apostles Peter and John came later to confirm them (Acts viii. 17). Thus, Holy Scripture teaches us that one becomes a Christian by baptism and that baptism is completed or sealed in confirmation; that baptism is administered with water in the name of the Father and the Son and the Holy Spirit. The sealing of the initiatory rite is by laying on of hands or anointing. This Christian Initiation is generally necessary for salvation and is intended for all people. Further, while baptism may be administered by anyone, minister or layman, confirmation is administered only by the Apostles or their successors.

Already in New Testament times a pattern was developing. First, people were instructed in the faith, as the eunuch was, or the jailer at Phillipi, renouncing their former ways, turning to God, then being baptized and confirmed. As we read in Hebrews (vi. 1, 2), these are "the rudiments of Christianity," that is, "repentance from the deadness of our former ways and faith in God, instruction about cleansing rites (baptism) and the laying on of hands." Here then is already a baptismal system existing in outline: The actual rite with the renunciation and profession, preceded by a preparation and followed by the Gift of the Spirit in confirmation. This structure is retained, in essence, right down to the present day. For example, the latest writings of the New Testament take us into the second century. At that time, as we have seen above, Christian Initiation consisted of (1) Instruction, (2) Renunciation of Evil, (3) Turning to God (Profession of Faith), and (4) Baptism (followed by Confirmation).

Let us examine the forms of baptism from the fourth century to the twentieth century and see the continuity of this structure.

First, we take a look at these elements (Renunciation, Profession of Faith and Baptism) as they are used in the Church in the fourth century. St. John Chrysostom set forth the basic form in a series of homilies delivered at Antioch between the years 386 and 398. He describes baptism as follows:

Renunciation

(At the renunciation, the candidate renounces Satan, his pomp, his service and his works, directing his renunciation at Satan, himself.)

"I renounce, you, Satan, and your pomp and your service and your works."

Profession of Faith

(The candidate, again speaking directly, turns to pledge himself to the service of Christ.)

"and I pledge myself to your service, Christ."

Anointing

(By the fourth century, the candidate was anointed after having renounced Satan and accepted Christ. This was done in the name of the Trinity.)

"The candidate is anointed in the Name of the Father and of the Son and, of the Holy Spirit."

Baptism

(Baptism was also administered in the name of the Trinity.)

"I baptize you in the Name of the Father and of the Son and of the Holy Spirit."

(Quotations from Chrysostom are taken from *Christian Initiation*, by Hugh M. Riley, pp. 30, 31, 147,) (Translation by author.)

A thousand years later we see that the form is little changed. We read from the Sarum Manual in the fourteenth century:

Renunciation

(By this time, the threefold renunciation spoken by the candidate, himself, now became answers to questions put by the priest. However, it is the same Renunciation.)

P. N., do you renounce Satan?

R. I renounce him.

P. And all his works?

R. I renounce them.

P. And all his pomps?

R. I renounce them.

Anointing

(In the Sarum use the Anointing came after the Renunciation but before the Profession of Faith. Further, the Anointing is in the name of Christ Jesus only and not the Holy Trinity.)

N., I sign you with oil in the name of Jesus Christ Our Lord; that you may have life eternal, and live unto the ages of ages, Amen.

Profession of Faith

(The Profession of Faith has now been expanded to include a threefold statement based on the Apostles' Creed. It also is now made in response to priestly questioning.)

P. N., do you believe in God the Father Almighty, creator of Heaven and Earth?

R. I believe.

P. Do you believe in Jesus Christ, his only Son Our Lord, who was born and suffered?

R. I believe.

P. Do you believe in the Holy Spirit, the Holy Catholic Church, the communion of Saints, the remission of sins, the resurrection of the body, and eternal life after death?

R. I believe.

Baptism

(The form is virtually unchanged, as the priest baptizes in the name of the Trinity.)

N., I baptize you in the name of the Father and of the Son and of the Holy Spirit, Amen.

(The language of the Sarum Manual is found in *A New History of the Book of Common Prayer,* by Procter and Frere, pp. 580, 581, 583, Translation by the author.)

Two hundred years later, the same form is adopted in the English *Book of Common Prayer* of 1549. For the first time the Anointing after the Renunciation is omitted. Otherwise, the rite remains essentially unchanged.

Renunciation

(This is still the threefold Renunciation seen in Chrysostom's Rite, but is in the Sarum form of question and answer.)

P. N., dost thou forsake the devil and all his works?

R. I forsake them.

P. Dost thou forsake the vain pomp and glory of the world, with all covetous desires of the same?

R. I forsake them.

P. Dost thou forsake all carnal desires of the flesh?

R. I forsake them.

Profession of Faith

(The threefold Profession is retained but expanded to include the entirety of the Apostle's Creed.

P. Dost thou believe in God the Father Almighty, maker of heaven and earth?

R. I believe.

P. And in Jesus Christ his only begotten son Our Lord? And that he was conceived by the Holy Ghost; born of the Virgin Mary; that he suffered under Pontius Pilate, was crucified, dead, and buried; that he went down into hell, and also did rise again the third day; that he ascended into heaven, and sitteth at the right hand of God the Father

Almighty; and from thence shall come again at the end of the world, to judge the quick and the dead?

R. I believe.

P. And dost thou believe in the Holy Ghost; the Holy Catholic Church; the Communion of Saints; the Remission of Sins; the Resurrection of the flesh; and everlasting life after death?

R. I believe.

Baptism

(Again, we see no basic change at all from the original Greek or the Latin.)

N., I baptize thee in the Name of the Father, and of the Son, and of the Holy Ghost. Amen.

The seventeenth century made only slight changes in the form. The anointing is still omitted. We now look at *The Book of Common Prayer* of 1662.

Renunciation

(The threefold Renunciation is now compressed into a single question and answer, retaining, however, the same rejection of the world, the flesh and the devil.)

P. Dost thou renounce the devil and all his works, the vain pomp and glory of the world, with all covetous desires of the same, and the carnal desires of the flesh, so that thou wilt not follow, nor be led by them?

R. I renounce them all.

Profession of Faith

(The Profession of Faith simply combines the threefold question into one question embracing the whole Apostles' Creed.)

P. Dost thou believe in God the Father Almighty, Maker of heaven and earth?
And in Jesus Christ his only-begotten Son Our Lord? And that he was conceived by the Holy Ghost; born of the Virgin Mary; that he suffered under Pontius Pilate, was crucified, dead and buried; that he went down into hell, and also did rise again the third day; that he ascended into heaven, and sitteth at the right hand of God the Father Almighty; and from thence shall come again at the end of the world, to judge the quick and the dead?
And dost thou believe in the Holy Ghost; the holy Catholic Church; the Communion of Saints; the Remission of sins; the Resurrection of the flesh; and everlasting life after death?

R. All this I steadfastly believe.

Baptism

(Again, no change.)

N., I baptize thee in the name of the Father, and of the Son, and of the Holy Ghost. Amen.

We move forward three centuries and across the Atlantic Ocean to the American *Book of Common Prayer* of 1928. The omission of the postrenunciation anointing has now been accepted as the norm.

Renunciation

(This is almost identical to the 1662 form.)

P. Dost thou renounce the devil and all his works, the vain pomp and glory of the world, with all covetous desires of the same, and the sinful desires of the flesh, so that thou wilt not follow, nor be led by them?

R. I renounce them all; and by God's help, will endeavor not to follow, nor be led by them.

Profession of Faith

(The lengthy recitation of the Apostles' Creed is replaced by a simpler threefold acceptance which includes a reference to the Creed.)

CHRISTIAN INITIATION

P. Dost thou believe in Jesus the Christ, the Son of the living God?

R. I do.

P. Dost thou accept him, and desire to follow him as thy Savior and Lord?

R. I do.

P. Dost thou believe all the Articles of the Christian Faith, as contained in the Apostles' Creed?

R. I do.

Baptism

(No change.)

N., I baptize thee in the name of the Father, and of the Son, and of the Holy Ghost. Amen.

The Episcopal Church in America has recently revised its Prayer Book. The new rites of Initiation do restore the use of chrism, but do not restore the renunciation anointing dropped in 1549. We examine the Rite as set forth in the 1979 *Book of Common Prayer.*

Renunciation

(The Rite returns to the threefold question and answer Renunciation form of 1549 and the Sarum Manual.)

P. Do you renounce Satan and all the spiritual forces of wickedness that rebel against God?

R. I renounce them.

P. Do you renounce the evil powers of this world which corrupt and destroy the creatures of God?

R. I renounce them.

P. Do you renounce all sinful desires that draw you from the love of God?

R. I renounce them.

Profession of Faith

(Again, the threefold acceptance of Christ, but the reference to the Apostles' Creed has been dropped. The form does provide a threefold question and answer statement of the Apostles' Creed as in 1549, but at a different place in the rite.)

P. Do you turn to Jesus Christ and accept him as your Savior?

R. I do.

P. Do you put your whole trust in his grace and love?

R. I do.

P. Do you promise to follow and obey him as your Lord?

R. I do

Baptism

(No change.)

N., I baptize you in the Name of the Father, and of the Son, and of the Holy Spirit. Amen.

So we can see a basic form and structure which has remained virtually unchanged from New Testament times, through the Reformation, right on down to the latest revisions of the rite.

But what about the doctrine of baptism? Has it been maintained intact, even as the form has? The answer must be yes: However, the thrust and emphasis of the Initiatory Rite has changed with the change in culture, custom and civilization.

The first real controversy arose over the question of the indelibility of baptism. While everyone recognized that baptism was not a repeatable act, many argued that baptism outside the Catholic Church was invalid and since it was void, the rebaptizing of heretics and schismatics was permitted. By the third century, Tertullian and Cyprian were arguing this position. However, the Church did not accept these arguments. In A.D. 314, the Council of Arles met in France (with British Bishops in attendance). At Arles, the Western Church recognized schismatic baptism. Eleven years later at the Council of Nicea, by Canon VIII, Novation baptism was recognized.

The final settlement grew out of St. Augustine of Hippo's dispute with the Donatists. The Donatists had revived Cyprian's objection to heterodox baptism. They further argued that heretical ministers could not validly baptize, on the theory that unworthy ministers lacked the Holy Spirit and could not give what they did not have. Augustine countered by declaring that those who received schismatic or heretical baptism nonetheless were validly baptized if there was the proper use of form, matter and intention. Further, he pointed out, concerning unworthy ministers that the true minister in every sacrament is Jesus Christ and that it is because of his agency that when the external requirements are rightly and seriously performed the promised operation of the Spirit is pledged. It is the Saviour's institution and promise rather than the earthly minister's faith and worthiness that makes the sacrament valid.

Augustine also argued that while heterodox baptism is valid, those baptized outside the Church receive the sacrament unworthily and do not benefit from it until they repent and submit to the Church. On such reconciliation the benefits of baptism are actualized. This is the doctrine of reviviscence.

Augustine finally stated that, as Scripture says baptism is for remission of sins and everyone, including infants, is stained with original sin, everyone, including infants, is to be baptized; that baptism is universally (generally) necessary to salvation. This does *not* mean that there is no hope at all for the unbaptized. To condemn to Hell those who have no real chance for baptism is a rash presumption denying the mercy of God. At least two classes of the unbaptized have been generally recognized as among the saved. These are (1) those who endured martyrdom for Christ's sake and (2) those who have wished to be baptized, but have had no real chance. They are commonly described as having received a baptism either of blood or desire. Moreover, the Church does not judge those who have no opportunity to know the good news of the Gospel of Christ.

Another issue is the relation of confirmation to baptism. In apostolic times the norm was to baptize and confirm at one and the same time although there were rare exceptions (e.g. Acts viii.). Since the apostle, or his successor, the bishop, was the minister of confirmation this meant that the bishop was the normal minister of the whole Initiatory Rite. At the earliest stages of Christian development this was no problem as the Church was small, with bishops in every center of Christianity. Further, the Church was in a real missionary situation and most persons to be baptized were adults. This meant that they were to undergo a long period of instruction before they would be baptized. Generally, they would be brought to the Bishop's Church for Initiation at Easter Eve.

By the fourth century, however, two factors had changed the emphasis of Initiation. In the first place, Christianity had become the established religion of the Roman Empire. As more and more people became Christian, fewer people were left for conversion and infant baptism, previously the exception, became the rule. Secondly, as the Church grew numerically and geographically it became more and more difficult to bring people to the bishop or for the bishop to go to all the Churches to baptize and confirm. Different solutions to the problem were reached in the East and the West.

The pattern in the East was to delegate to the priest the authority to confirm, maintaining episcopal contact with the Rite by requiring the priest to use chrism blessed by the bishop for the confirmation. An example of this is seen in the fourth century Apostolic Constitutions, VII. 28, which allowed presbyters to confirm with Episcopally blessed oil. This is still the practice in the Orthodox Church. By this method, the former practice of one Initiatory Rite was preserved.

At first the West appeared to follow the same development. In A.D. 400, at the Council of Toledo in Spain, priests were authorized to confirm with oil blessed by the bishop. However, there was still the problem of those baptized by a deacon or a layman. Only the priest or bishop could confirm. The Council of Elvira (A.D. 305) had provided in the case of lay baptism (Canon 38) and deacon's baptism (Canon 77) that the person so baptized was to be brought to the bishop for confirmation as soon as practical. This still allowed for priests to confirm. Further, at Rome, the bishop still retained the right to confirm, even if the priest baptized. St. Jerome wrote, in A.D. 379 *(Dialogue Against the Luciferians,* chapter 9) in regard to Western practice, "It is the custom of the church that the bishop should rush about to those who have been baptized by presbyters and deacons far from the larger cities, to invoke the Holy Spirit upon them by the laying on of hands."

Pope Gregory the Great, in A.D. 593, began to limit the authority of priests to confirm. He wrote to the Archbishop of Sardinia that the anointing of the newly baptized on the forehead (confirmation) was to be reserved to the bishop. Because of great opposition to this, he later allowed priests to confirm, but only if a bishop was not available.

From this time on, confirmation in the West became the normal province of the bishop, although on rare occasions, and for exceptional emergencies, priestly confirmation was allowed. It was conceded by Pope Eugenius IV, at the Council of Florence in 1439, (Decree for the Armenians) that for urgent reasons, and by papal dispensation, priests could administer the chrism of confirmation. But a century later the Council of Trent (Session VII) reiterated the doctrine that a bishop is the sole "ordinary" minister of confirmation. Thus, because of the insistence on confirmation by the bishop in the West, baptism and confirmation became separated by both time and place. This separation began to become common by the eighth century and canon law began to try to keep the separation from being too great. The English Canon Law of 960 stated:

> "We teach that each priest perform baptism as soon as it is required. And then let him enjoin his parish that each infant be baptized within 37 days, and that no one too long remain unbishopped."

(Compare this to the rubric in the 1928 Prayer Book, page 281:

> "It is expedient that every Adult, thus baptized, should be confirmed by the Bishop, so soon after his Baptism as conveniently may be . . . ")

Because of the separation of baptism and confirmation and because of infrequent episcopal visitations, many people were admitted to communion without confirmation. Indeed, confirmation was on the verge of being totally neglected and ignored. In view of the doctrine that confirmation is the complement of baptism and therefore an important part of the full spiritual qualification for reception of communion, the admission to communion without confirmation was regarded as an abuse. Archbishop Peckham of Canterbury, in his *Constitution of 1281*, decreed, "No one who is not in peril of death shall be admitted to the Sacrament of the Body and Blood of the Lord unless he be confirmed or has been reasonably hindered from being confirmed." This was subsequently made a rubric in the Baptismal Rite of the Sarum Manual and then adapted to the Prayer Book, "And there shall none be admitted to the Holy Communion, until such time as he be confirmed, or be ready and desirous to be confirmed."

What of the form of confirmation? The common form in New Testament times was by laying on of hands. There were the few references to "anointing" but imposition of hands was the standard. By the early third century, the form includes both anointing and the laying on of hands. For example, Tertullian describes Christian Initiation as consisting of baptism, then three distinct rites, an anointing, a signing on the forehead, and finally a laying on of hands *(De baptismo,* 8).

By the late fourth century, the rite was reduced to a consignation or chrismation with oil. (Oddly, Chrysostom does not even mention a postbaptismal anointing.) The laying on of hands gradually was overshadowed by this chrismation. Even in the West, by the fifteenth century, the laying on of hands was largely symbolic and it was not until the sixteenth century that Anglicans returned to the traditional, Scriptural form of confirmation.

While the Anglican Church had returned to the ancient tradition of the laying on of hands, there had been a subtle change in emphasis. During the Protestant Reformation, the Calvinists rejected confirmation as "an invented sacrament." Further, except for the Lutherans in Scandinavia, the Protestants had abolished the episcopacy, thus destroying the officer of confirmation. However, the Reformers saw the need for what John Calvin called "a catechetical exercise, in which children or youths (would) deliver an account of their faith in the presence of the Church." Protestant "confirmation," administered by local ministers, became widely used as the occasion on which an instructed young Christian, who had been baptized in infancy, makes a public witness to his faith and accepts the duties and privileges of adult church membership.

The Anglican Church combined both the Pre-Reformation view of confirmation as the completion or seal of baptism and the Protestant view of confirmation as a re-affirmation of the faith already received. Baptism was considered as the rite of Initiation into the Christian Church, normally for infants, followed by catechism or instruction in the faith as soon as the baptized person was old enough. Confirmation then came, both as a completion of the baptismal act and as an occasion for the affirmation of the baptismal faith. This was followed by First Communion. Thus, the ancient Initiatory Rite was preserved (i.e. Baptism, Confirmation, Communion), but now was separated into three distinct parts. The rubrics of the 1928 Prayer Book indicate this separation. For example, after baptism, the rubric urges that the "baptized should be confirmed by the Bishop, so soon after his baptism as conveniently may be." The rubric after confirmation directs the priest "to move the persons confirmed to come, without delay, to the Lord's Supper"; all implying that no one part necessarily immediately joined another part. (By contrast, the 1979 Prayer Book moves toward a restoration of Baptism, Confirmation and Eucharist as a unity, pp. 299-310.)

While the ancient unity was still recognized (Queen Elizabeth was baptized, confirmed and communicated in infancy in 1534), it was not generally practiced. Only the continuity of the order remained.

We can note the changes made between the Ante-Nicene practice and the Post-Reformation practice. In the early Church, Christian Initiation was preceded by a long period of instruction before any part of the rite was administered. In the Post-Reformation Anglican branch of the Church, the instruction, or catechism, came after the baptismal rite and before confirmation. This was largely because adults were the normal recipients of Ante-Nicene baptism and infants of Post-Reformation baptism. In the early Church, the whole rite was normally administered in a single service of baptism, confirmation and communion. In the later Church, the rite was separated into different parts, administered at different times.

While there have been these changes, there is a remarkable continuity of form and content over the past two thousand years. There is also a continuity of doctrine in the Sacraments. We are told, concerning the form and matter of baptism, in the catechism:

"Q. What is the outward and visible sign in Baptism?

A. The outward and visible sign in Baptism is water, in which the person is baptized, *In the Name of the Father, and of the Son, and of the Holy Spirit"* (Prayer Book, p. 858).

We are further told that we receive a spiritual grace, which is "union with Christ in his death and resurrection, birth into God's family the Church, forgiveness of sins, and new life in the Holy Spirit." Also, we must "renounce Satan, repent of our sins, and accept Jesus as our Lord and Savior."

Infant baptism is practiced so that "they can share citizenship in the Covenant, membership in Christ, and redemption by God." This is possible through the promises of parents and sponsors "who guarantee that the infants will be brought up within the Church, to know Christ and be able to follow him."

In regard to the wholeness of Christian Initiation, for the strength to do the Will of God, the Prayer Book says (P. 860):

"Q. What is Confirmation?

A. Confirmation is the rite in which we express a mature commitment to Christ, and receive strength from the Holy Spirit through prayer and the laying on of hands by a bishop."

Further, we are told that Baptism and the Eucharist are "ordained of Christ Our Lord in the Gospel" as "sacraments" (Article XXV, Articles of Religion), and that confirmation is one of the rites "commonly called sacraments," but that unlike baptism, Our Lord did not ordain "any particular sign or ceremony" for it (ibid). As to the questions raised to St. Augustine on the personal worthiness of the minister affecting the validity of the sacrament, the Church says (Article XXVI):

"Although in the visible Church the evil be ever mingled with the good, and sometimes the evil have chief authority in the Ministration of the Word and Sacraments, yet forasmuch as they do not the same in their own name, but in Christ's, and do minister by his commission and authority, we may use their Ministry, both in hearing the Word of God, and in receiving the Sacraments. Neither is the effect of Christ's ordinance taken away by their wickedness, nor the grace of God's gifts diminished from such as by faith, and rightly, do receive the Sacraments ministered unto them; which be effectual, because of Christ's institution and promise, although they be ministered by evil men."

Finally, the Church says (Article XXVII):

"Baptism is not only a sign of profession, and mark of difference, whereby Christian men are discerned from others that be not christened, but it is also a sign of Regeneration of New-Birth, whereby as by an instrument, they that receive Baptism rightly are grafted into the Church; the promises of the forgiveness of sin, and of our adoption to be the sons of God by the Holy Ghost, are visibly signed and sealed; Faith is confirmed, and Grace increased by virtue of prayer unto God.

"The Baptism of young Children is in any wise to be retained in the Church, as most agreeable with the institution of Christ."

CHAPTER 5

The Eucharist

Having seen in the last chapter that Baptism is entrance into the Body of Christ, we now turn to the Eucharist. What we do believe concerning this Holy Sacrament?

First, this Sacrament is commanded of the Church. "Do this" Our Lord directs the apostles when he institutes the Eucharist. Moreover, he expected the Eucharist to be an essential part of Christian practice. Experience has proved that no one can long sustain a spiritual life who deliberately turns his back on the Lord's Table. Therefore, Our Lord, knowing what was in man, said, "Except ye eat the flesh of the Son of Man and drink his blood, ye have no life in you (Jn. vi. 53)."

The Old Testament may not be disregarded in any proper study of the Eucharist; for, as in other subjects, Our Lord gave his eucharistic teaching based upon the background of the Old Covenant. In particular its sacrificial rites, which were fulfilled on the Cross, also point to the pure offering of the New Covenant. As the author of the Epistle to the Hebrews said:

"The first Covenant indeed had its ordinances of divine service and its sanctuary, but a material sanctuary. For a tent was prepared — the first Presence; this is called the Holy Place. Beyond the second curtain was the tent called the Most Holy Place. Here was a golden altar of incense, and ark of the covenant plated all over with gold, in which were a golden jar containing the manna, and Aaron's staff which once budded, and the tablets of the covenant; and above it the cherubim of God's glory, overshadowing the place of expiation (Heb. ix. 1-5)." (See also Exod. xxv.-xxvi.)

"But now Christ has come, high priest of good things already in being. The tent of his priesthood is a greater and more perfect one, not made by men's hands, that is, not belonging to this created world; the blood of his sacrifice is his own blood, not the blood of goats and calves; and thus he has entered the sanctuary once and for all and secured an eternal deliverance. For if the blood of goats and bulls and the sprinkled ashes of a heifer have power to hallow those who have been defiled and restore their external purity, how much greater is the power of the blood of Christ; he offered himself without blemish to God, a spiritual and eternal sacrifice; and his blood will cleanse our conscience from the deadness of our former ways and fit us for the service of the living God (Heb. ix. 11-14)."

The Eucharist is this offering of the sacrifice of Christ and in it what the older ritual prefigured comes to be truly represented and effectively applied; a sacrifice once for all accomplished, but living on both in Christ's Heavenly intercession and in the earthly and Eucharistic memorial. As St. Paul said: "For every time you eat this bread and drink the cup, you proclaim the death of the Lord, until he comes (1 Cor. xi. 26)." Because it is the memorial of Christ's death, in which all previous sacrifices are summed up, and because it completely fills the place in the New Covenant which these sacrifices occupied in the Old, it is likewise in a representative way a fulfilment of the various mysteries which the sacrifices of Israel foreshadowed.

The Eucharist is also an offering of bread and wine. The manna (heavenly bread) with which the Israelites were miraculously fed during their forty years of wandering in the wilderness is the starting point of Our Lord's discourse in John's Gospel on the Bread from Heaven which he was to give. The giving of the manna is recorded in Exodus (Exod. xvi. 14-15), and the direction to preserve a jar of it in the "presence of the Lord" (see Hebrews above) is found at Exod. xvi. 33. Seizing upon his listeners' reference to the giving of manna from heaven in the wilderness, Our Lord tells them that the Father gives true bread, "The bread of God cometh down from Heaven and giveth life unto the world (Jn. vi. 33)" and claims Himself to be this bread of life in which all must believe who would have eternal life and be raised by Him at the last day.

He proceeds to reaffirm this as against the Jews' murmuring and says:

> "I am the living bread which came out of heaven: If any man eat of this bread, he shall live forever: Yea, in the bread which I will give is my flesh, for the life of the world ... Verily, verily, I say unto you, except you eat the flesh of the son of man and drink his blood, you have not life in yourselves. He that eateth my flesh and drinketh my blood hath eternal life; and I will raise him up at the last day. For my flesh is meat indeed, and my blood is drink indeed. He that eateth my flesh and drinketh my blood abideth in me, and I in him. As the living Father has sent me, and I live because of the Father; so he that eateth me, he also shall live because of me. This is the bread which came down out of heaven: Not as the fathers did eat manna and died: He that eateth this bread shall live forever (Jn. vi. 51, 53-58)."

This prefiguring of the Eucharist caused great consternation among his followers. However, rather than give them some simple explanation, he said to them, "The words that I have spoken unto you are spirit, and are life (Jn. vi. 63.)." This explanation, since it appeared to leave unreduced the teaching that they must partake of his Flesh and Blood failed to satisfy many of those disciples who walked no more with him (Jn. vi. 66). The apostles themselves were concerned about this; Our Lord even asked them if they wished to leave him (Jn. vi. 67). It was not until his institution of the Holy Eucharist at the Last Supper on the night before he was betrayed, that they began to understand what he meant by eating his Flesh and drinking his Blood.

The Old Covenant had been sealed with blood of the sacrifice (Exod. xxiv. 6-8); the New Covenant was likewise sealed with the blood of sacrifice (Heb. ix. 12, 15). After the shedding of blood at the institution of the first Covenant, the elders of Israel ate the sacrifice in the presence of God (Exod. xxiv. 12; xxix. 31-33). Likewise, the Flesh of the Sacrificial Victim of the New Covenant was to be eaten by the faithful (Jn. vi. 53).

The earliest New Testament account of the institution of the Eucharist is given by St. Paul, in his First Epistle to the Corinthians. In this passage we have a specific reference to the sacrificial blood of covenant, harking back to the covenant of Exodus:

> "The Lord Jesus in the night in which he was betrayed took bread; and when he had given thanks, he brake it, and said, this is my body which is for you: This do for my memorial. In like manner also the cup after supper, saying, this cup is the new covenant in my blood: This do, as oft as ye drink it, for my memorial (1 Cor. xi. 23-25)."

Of course blood involves the offering of a sacrifice and the death of a sacrificial victim. The Gospel accounts of the institution are set in that context of the impending Sacrifice of the Cross. In Matthew's Gospel, for example, we have the record of the institution of the Eucharist:

> "During supper Jesus took bread, and having said the blessing he broke it and gave it to the disciples with the words: 'Take this and eat; this is my body.' Then he took a cup, and having offered thanks to God he gave it to them with the words: 'Drink from it, all of you. For this is my blood, the blood of the covenant, shed for many for the forgiveness of sins' (Matt. xxvi. 26-28)."

Immediately following this account Jesus refers to his death and resurrection (Matt. xxvi. 31, 32).

So also Mark:

> "During supper he took bread, and having said the blessing he broke it and gave it to them, with the words: 'Take this; this is my body.' Then he took a cup, and having offered thanks to God he gave it to them; and they all drank from it. And he said, 'This is my blood, the blood of the covenant, shed for many'. . . And Jesus said, 'You will all fall from your faith; for it stands written: "I will strike the shepherd down and the sheep will be scattered." Nevertheless, after I am raised again I will go on before you into Galilee' (Mk. xiv. 22-24, 27-29)."

Luke is even more explicit in his reference to the betrayal and death of Christ:

> "And he took bread, gave thanks, and broke it; and he gave it to them, with the words: 'This is my body which is

given for you; do this as a memorial of me.' In the same way he took the cup after supper, and said, 'This cup, poured out for you, is the new covenant sealed by my blood.' 'But mark this — my betrayer is here, his hand with mine on the table. For the Son of Man is going his appointed way' (Lk. xx. 19-22)."

The sacrifice of Christ on the Cross draws to mind the immediate parallel with the proffered sacrifice of Isaac. In the twenty-second chapter of Genesis we are given the account of God directing Abraham to take his only legitimate son, Isaac, and to offer him as a sacrifice. Abraham abides by the word of God, takes his only son into the wilderness, builds an altar and is prepared to offer Isaac as a sacrifice to God. At the last minute the angel of the Lord intervenes and tells Abraham, "Do not raise your hand against the boy: Do not touch him. Now I know that you are a God fearing man. You have not withheld from me your son, you only son (Gen. xx. 12)." While God would not allow Abraham to sacrifice his only son for the sins of the world, the Father was willing to allow his Only Begotten Son, Jesus Christ, to be so sacrificed on the cross.

St. Paul also draws the clear parallel between the sacrifice of Christ and the sacrifice of the Passover when the paschal lamb is offered to protect the Jewish people from the Angel of Death: "For indeed our Passover has begun; the sacrifice is offered — Christ himself (1 Cor. v. 7)." (See also Exodus, xii. 7, 8, in which the paschal victim is eaten.) The offering of this sacrifice, the Celebration of the Holy Eucharist, was an essential part of the life of the Church. We are told in Holy Scripture that the early Christians met constantly to break bread; that is, to offer the Eucharistic Sacrifice (Acts ii. 42). Even in New Testament times it was customary to offer the Eucharist and to worship on the Lord's Day (Acts xx. 7; 1 Cor. xvi. 2; Rev. i. 10).

The Church recognized that in the Eucharist Christ was in a very real way present and there was a danger to those souls who failed to recognize the Presence of the Lord therein. St. Paul, therefore, points out that we must involve ourselves in self-examination before we receive the Eucharist:

"Wherefore, whosoever shall eat this bread, and drink this cup of the Lord unworthily, shall be guilty of the body and blood of the Lord. But let a man examine himself and so let him eat of that bread and drink of that cup. For he that eateth and drinketh unworthily, eateth and drinketh damnation to himself, not discerning the Lord's body (l Cor. xi. 27-29)."

Again, Scripture draws for us the parallel between the Old Testament sacrifices and the sacrifice offered once and for all for the remission of sins by Our Lord and Saviour on the Cross, as in the Epistle to the Hebrews:

"Every high priest is appointed to offer gifts and sacrifices; hence, this one too must have something to offer. Now if he had been on earth, he would not even have been a priest, since there are already priests who offer the gifts which the Law prescribes, though they minister in a sanctuary which is only a copy and shadow of the heavenly. . . . But in fact the ministry which has fallen to Jesus is as far superior to theirs as are the covenant he mediates and the promises upon which it is legally secured.

* * *

"If, then, these sacrifices cleanse the copies of heavenly things, those heavenly things themselves require better sacrifices to cleanse them. For Christ has entered, not that sanctuary made by men's hands which is only a symbol of the reality, but heaven itself, to appear now before God on our behalf. . . . (H)e has appeared once and for all at the climax of history to abolish sin by the sacrifice of himself (Heb. viii. 3-5a, 6; ix. 23-24, 26)."

It is important to note that the author points out the eternal nature of Our Lord's sacrifice and reminds us that Christ is both priest and victim, offering himself upon the altar of the cross before God on our behalf, an offering made once and for all. In this Epistle the author refers to the priesthood of Melchizedek and the proffered sacrifice of Isaac by Abraham as well as the sacrifices of the Old Testament as types and shadows of the New. Moreover, as St. Paul said:

"For every time you eat this bread and drink the cup, you proclaim the death of the Lord, until he comes (l Cor. xi. 27)."

Finally, the New Testament Church saw in the Eucharist a foretaste of the worship of God in Heaven as described in the Book of Revelation:

> "Then the angel said to me, 'Write this: "Happy are those who are invited to the wedding-supper of the Lamb!" ' (Rev. xix. 9)."

> "Then one of the seven angels . . . came and spoke to me and said, 'Come, and I will show you the bride, the wife of the Lamb.' So in the Spirit he carried me away to a great high mountain, and showed me the holy city of Jerusalem coming down out of heaven from God . . . . I saw no temple in the city; for its temple was the sovereign Lord God and the Lamb . . . . The throne of God and of the Lamb will be there, and his servants shall worship him; they shall see him face to face, and bear his name on their foreheads (Rev. xxi. 9, 10, 22; xxii. 3)."

> " 'Come!' say the Spirit and the bride. 'Come!' let each hearer reply. Come forward, you who are thirsty; accept the water of life, a free gift to all who desire it (Rev. xxii. 17)."

And in the messianic banquet as prophesied by Isaiah:

> "On this mountain the Lord of Hosts will prepare a banquet of rich fare for all the peoples, a banquet of wines well matured and richest fare, well-matured wines strained clear. On this mountain the Lord will swallow up that veil that shrouds all the peoples, the pall thrown over all the nations; he will swallow up death for ever (Isa. xxv. 6-8)."

And so we see the Eucharist described as "heavenly food," the "Body and Blood" of Christ, a rite signifying the offering of Christ upon Calvary as a sacrifice for our sins, a sacrifice that swallows up death. From this the Church developed two statements: (1) The Eucharist is a sacrifice, and (2) Christ is truly present in the Eucharist. Let us then take a look at the beliefs of the early Church Fathers concerning the Eucharist as sacrifice and the Presence of Christ therein.

The *Didache* uses the term "sacrifice" to describe the Eucharist. Justin Martyr, writing in the second century, spoke of "all the sacrifices in this name which Jesus appointed to be performed as in the Eucharist of the Bread and the Cup, and which are celebrated in every place by Christians . . . The Bread of the Eucharist and the Cup likewise of the Eucharist (are indentified with) the sacrifice foretold by Malachi." Justin Martyr goes on to say "we do not receive these as common bread or a common drink. But just as Our Saviour Jesus Christ was made flesh through the word of God and had both flesh and blood for our salvation, so also we have been taught that the food which has been eucharistized by the word of prayer from Him (that food by which process of assimilation nourishes our flesh and blood) is the flesh and blood of the incarnate Jesus."

Ignatius declared that "the Eucharist is the flesh of Our Saviour Jesus Christ, which suffered for our sins and which the Father in His goodness raised."

In the writings of St. Augustine we find the Bishop of Hippo following Tertullian and St. Cyprian in stating a belief in the objective Real Presence of the Body and Blood of Christ, which was the offering and the heart of Christian worship.

In the late fourth century, we read the words of St. Gregory of Nyssa:

> "The bread sanctified by the Word of God we believe to be transmuted into the Body of God the Word.
>
> "So man by a sort of union with that which is of immortality becomes a sharer in incorruption."

St. Ambrose, a contemporary of St. Gregory, wrote:

> "And whenever we receive the sacrament which is transfigured through the mystery of holy prayer into flesh and blood, we show forth the Lord's death."
>
> "We have seen the High Priest coming to us, we have seen and heard Him offering His Blood for us. We follow as we are able, we priests in offering the sacrifice for the people."

So we can see a clear cut belief in the sacrifice and the Real Presence of Our Lord in the Sacrament from New Testament times right on down to the end of the fourth century and

THE EUCHARIST

beyond. However, in the earlier period, the sacrifice seen in the Eucharist is identified, first as the fulfillment of the Old Testament sacrifices (e.g. Hebrews) and later an offering of the first fruits as in the offertory of bread and wine (e.g. Irenaeus). Justin, Ambrose and St. Gregory are moving in the direction of the sacrifices as related to Christ's death on the cross and the offering of the bread and wine that they may be for us the Body and Blood of Christ.

Having examined the theological developments of the early ages of the Church, let us now look at the liturgical foundations of the Eucharist. For that purpose we must return to the New Testament period and the Last Supper. While some authorities have attempted to equate the Last Supper with the Passover (because of its proximity to the actual Passover and Our Lord's crucifixion), a more accurate view seems to be that Our Lord was gathering in the upper room with his Apostles for a fellowship meal and not the Passover. This view is expressed in *Liturgy and Worship*, in the Eucharistic Section by Frank Gavin:

"The generally held theory of the chronology of the Passion, and the Pauline assimilation of the cycle of Passover ideas to the Passion (Cf. I. Cor. v. 7-8), have until fairly recently led scholars to find the background of the Last Supper in the Jewish Passover. Against this view it may be urged: That there was no lamb, nor the use of the liturgical narrative of the Passover; it is 'bread,' not 'unleavened bread,' which is used; and there is but one cup, not the four prescribed by the Jewish ritual. The supper could not have been even an adaptation of the Passover."

Gavin goes on to refer to a fellowship meeting within the framework of a *Kiddush*, a quasi-religious meal on the eve of a Sabbath or major feast.

Dom Gregory Dix, in *The Shape of the Liturgy*, arrives at the same conclusion:

"Our Lord instituted the Eucharist at a supper with his Disciples which was probably *not* the Passover Supper of that year, but the evening meal 24 hours before the actual Passover. On this St. John appears to contradict the other three Gospels, and it seems that St. John is right.

Nevertheless, from what occurred at it and from the way in which it was regarded by the primitive Jewish Christian Church it is evident that the Last Supper was a Jewish 'religious meal' of some kind. The type to which it best conforms is the formal supper of a *chaburah*."

A variant of the word *chaburah* is found in Frank Gavin's article on the Eucharist when he refers to 'fellowships' *(haburoth)*.

This same conclusion was reached by the Standing Liturgical Commission of the Episcopal Church in Prayer Book Studies IV, *The Eucharistic Liturgy:*

"Since the Jewish family meal was always a religious occasion, it embodied a fixed ritual, always observed when friends and neighbors met at such a *Chaburah* or 'meal of fellowship' (from *chaber* 'neighbor') as was the Last Supper."

It was the Jewish custom to partake of no food without a prayer of blessing, by way of thanksgiving to God. Thus, at a *chaburah* meal, the supper begins with grace before meals. If there were any relishes or appetizers before a meal, there would have been a blessing said over the relishes by each of the guests, and if there had been wine before the meal, each would have said a blessing over his own cup of wine. The meal proper begins, however, with the blessing and breaking of bread. The breaking of the single loaf of bread and the sharing of it demonstrates the unity of the "friends" *(chaberim)*. Our Lord would have given thanks over the bread in approximately these words:

"Blessed be Thou, O Lord Our God, Eternal King,
   Who bringest forth bread from the earth."

However, at the distribution he adds something not in the old Jewish ritual: "This is my Body which is given for you. Do this for the recalling of me." Thereafter, supper continues with the regular course of food. At last, at the end of the meal, there is a ritual washing of hands. (It is probably at this point that Our Lord washed the feet of his disciples.) Following the washing, comes the final benediction said after all meals. At a chaburah supper, this would be said over a "cup of blessing" a cup of wine mixed with a little water.

The benediction has been preserved in Jewish literature,

beginning with versicles and responses between the host and the guests, and then continues: "Blessed art Thou, O Lord Our God, Eternal King, who feedest the whole world with Thy Goodness, with grace, with loving kindness and with tender mercy." The prayer continues for several paragraphs of thanksgiving and prayer for mercy. Having blessed the cup of wine, Our Lord gave it to them and they all drank of it. However, while the cup was being passed from one to another in silence, Our Lord adds the following language: "This Cup is the New Testament in my Blood. Do this whenever you drink it for the remembrance of me."

It should be noted that the above description of the chaburah meal, with the insertion of Our Lord's words, comports with the abbreviated descriptions given in Scripture. Especially this is true when we see the reference to two different cups of wine in St. Luke's narrative, one before the meal and one after.

After Our Lord's Resurrection, the Christian community everywhere followed the injunction to "do this" (Acts ii. 42). Apparently, at first, the "breaking of the bread," as the Eucharist is often referred to in the New Testament, was celebrated in conjuction with a supper, as Our Lord has done. However, this led to certain abuses (I Cor. xi.). Consequently, St. Paul points out the dangers of the combined supper (agapé) and the "breaking of bread" (Eucharist). We therefore find that the Eucharist and the agapé become separated into two different services before the end of the Apostolic age. In that "breaking of bread," we see a definite action. The action done in the Eucharist was a sevenfold one:

1. The bread is taken.

2. The bread is blessed.

3. The bread is broken.

4. The bread is given.

5. The cup is taken.

6. The cup is blessed.

7. The cup is given.

Prior to the removal of the agapé from the Eucharist, this sevenfold action was separated with the first four parts coming before the meal proper and the last three coming afterwards. When the meal, or *agapé* was separated from the actions, the "doing" with the bread and the wine became conjoint and the Eucharist then took on the historic "fourfold shape."

The president of the Eucharist would:

1. Take the bread and the cup.

2. Bless the bread and the cup.

3. Break the bread.

4. Give the bread and the cup.

These four actions are respectively enacted in the four great acts of the liturgy as follows:

1. The Offertory.

2. The Prayer of Blessing or Consecration.

3. The Fraction.

4. The Communion.

This fourfold shape was known as the Eucharist, from the Greek *eucharistia* (thanksgiving).

A second service which was sometimes used in conjuction with the Eucharist and sometimes used apart from it, was service of Scripture reading and preaching, known as the Synaxis. This is a service developed from the synagogue services of Scripture reading, explanation and prayer. The basic form is:

1. Opening greeting by the officiant.

2. Lessons, separated by psalmody.

3. Sermon.

4. Dismissal of those who did not belong to the Church.

5. Prayers for the faithful and final dismissal.

By the second century the Synaxis and the Eucharist are joined into a single service. (However, the tradition remained of omitting the Synaxis in such instances as Baptism, which replaced the Synaxis, followed by the Eucharist, beginning at the Offertory. This same ancient pattern is reflected in the 1979 *Book of Common Prayer* of the Episcopal Church for special occasions such as Baptism, Confirmation, Marriage and Burial. The Synaxis, by itself, survives as Ante-Communion.)

This basic structure and form is to be seen in the entire Christian Church by the end of the third and beginning of the fourth centuries. It should be noted, however, that there is no real evidence to show that the liturgy was framed in specific words that were universally accepted throughout the Church. To the contrary, it appears that there was a basic unified form, as outlined above, with the actual wording of prayers and thanksgivings left up to the individual celebrants. In the first century and well into the second, the bishop, as successor of the apostle, was the normal celebrant at the Eucharist. It is only as the Church grows out of the cities and expands into a number of local congregations that the authority to celebrate the Eucharist is delegated by the bishop to parish priests. It should further be borne in mind that the Church was, until the first decades of the fourth century, a private group suffering from severe persecution. Because of this the Eucharist was celebrated primarily in private homes with as little fanfare as possible. Moreover, the Eucharist was seen in an eschatological way, looking forward to the "heavenly banquet" to come.

As the Church emerged from the period of persecution, the liturgy underwent expansion and change with the addition of ceremonial as worship became public. While we do not have space here to explore this change in detail, we should note the great liturgies of Alexandria, Jerusalem, Antioch and Byzantium in the East, and the Roman liturgy in the West. There was considerable borrowing among these varied centers and certain things were gradually added to the basic Eucharistic structure as outlined above. For example, in the East, the Eucharistic prayer began to center upon the Invocation of the Holy Spirit, while in the West the emphasis was upon the Words of Institution. The Sanctus and Lord's Prayer were added to the Eucharist, as were the Agnus Dei and the Gloria in excelsis. An opening litany was gradually displaced by the

Kyrie. The simple use of incense in the procession of the president of the Eucharist, as in the magistrates of Rome, became the liturgical use of incense. The practical use of candles to provide light for the readers became the symbolic use of candles to symbolize Christ as the Light of the World. Processions, the glorious singing of trained choirs as opposed to the simple chant of the early Church and other changes were introduced with the freeing up of the Church from the strictures of persecution and prohibition.

In the West, the Roman liturgy gradually displaced other rites so that by the eve of the Reformation, the Roman Rite in its different varieties was the standard structure of Eucharistic worship for the entire West. In England there were numerous variants of the Roman Rite. The most influential, of course, was the Sarum Rite and it is at this point that we take a look at the development of Anglican Eucharistic theology and liturgy.

The shift in emphasis from the eschatological viewpoint of the early centuries — a looking forward to the "last things" — to the seeing of the Eucharist as a representation of the Sacrifice of Christ on the Cross — a looking back to an earlier event — laid the ground work for real controversies during the Reformation. The early Church had seen the Eucharist as a foretaste of the Messianic banquet and a foretaste of our worship of God in Heaven as prophesied by Isaiah. By the fourteenth and fifteenth centuries, however, with the emphasis on looking back to the Sacrifice of Calvary, the Eucharistic viewpoint became very narrow and centered on the two issues mentioned: (1) The Eucharistic Sacrifice; (2) The Real Presence. The doctrine of the Eucharistic Sacrifice was, itself, narrowed even further to the question of whether the sacrifice of the altar was a new offering of the Sacrifice on the Cross to placate God; that is, a propitiation for sins. Thus we find the medieval writers refering to a propitiatory sacrifice.*
It was against this viewpoint that the English reforms were to protest violently.

---

*(It should be noted that the use of the term "propitiatory sacrifice" in the sixteenth century refers to two things: (1) The Sacrifice of the Cross is to appease or placate an angry God, and (2) Christ is offered anew as such a sacrifice in each Eucharist. Actually, the Greek work *hilasmos* translated "propitiation" in the King James Version (l Jn. ii. 2) is more properly translated "expiation," that is, an offering for sin, with no concept of appeasement.

The *medieval* concept of "propitiatory sacrifice" taught that in the Eucharist there is not only the sacrifice of "praise and thanksgiving" but a real sacrifice of Christ. Many authors declared that the priest sacrifices Christ anew in each Mass. It was argued that if one sacrifice was good, then many sacrifices were better. Thus, private Masses would be offered on behalf of a particular person or for a particular purpose. The more Masses, the more grace poured out for the person or purpose. Of course, this meant that the mere *act* of offering was the most important thing in the Mass. Communion, the original purpose of the Sacrament, was so low a priority that virtually no one made his communion. Instead, people went to Mass to see the elevation of the host: "Seeing" their Lord was more important than receiving him.

It was against this concept of propitiatory sacrifice that the Anglican Reformers revolted. The Anglican fathers desired to return to the concept of the Eucharist as it had been in the early days of the Church; to recapture the Biblical viewpoint, together with a regular communion on the part of the people, and to reaffirm that the Sacrifice on the cross is the sole sacrifice for our sins.

In the sixteenth century we see this viewpoint of the propitiatory sacrifice set forth by Stephen Gardiner, pro-Roman Bishop of Winchester. He stated, in his lengthy correspondence with Archbishop Cranmer, that Christ instituted as a remembrance of his own sacrifice:

> "the presence of the same most precious substance to be ... sacrificed by the priests, to be the pure sacrifice of the church there offered for the effect of increase of life in us, as it was offered on the cross to achieve life unto us ... By this sacrifice, once after the order of Melchisedech, Christ's death is not iterate, but a memory daily renewed of that death ... but in such wise as the same body is offered on the altar of the cross; but the same

---

Christ was the "perfect offering" for sin, or made "atonement." The twentieth century use of the word "propitiation" is understood to mean "expiation," rather than the sixteenth century concept of winning God's favor. The Eucharist, insofar as it is a commemoration of the Sacrifice of the Cross, is a re-presentation of that expiation or perfect offering. In that modern sense the Eucharistiac Sacrifice can be called "propitiatory," but it does not mean the same thing as our sixteenth century forebears understood by the term.)

manner of offering is not daily that was on the altar of the cross, for the daily offering is without bloodshed, and is termed so to signify that bloodshedding once done to be sufficient."

Gardiner goes on to say that this is a sacrifice and an oblation:

"because it is a memory and representation of the true sacrifice and holy immolation done at the altar of the cross. And Christ was once dead on the cross and there was offered in himself; but he is daily immolate in the sacrament because in the sacrament there is made a memory of that is once done."

He then continues:

"Thus writeth Petrus Lombardus, whose judgment because this author (i.e. Cranmer) alloweth he must grant the visible church hath priests in ministry, that offer daily Christ's most precious body and blood in mystery; and then must it be granted, that Christ so offered Himself in His supper; for otherwise than He did cannot be done now. And by the judgment of Petrus Lombardus the same most precious body and blood is offered daily, that once suffered and was once shed."

Richard Smith, another pro-Romanist writer, in response to Cranmer, states:

"We affirm and teach that He Himself offereth His body and Blood daily at Mass by the ministry of the priest as He doth continually baptize and preach unto the people by His ministers the priests."

In another passage he states:

"The Mass must needs be a sacrifice, wherein He is continually sacrificed by the priests, His ministers, after the order of Melchizedech."

Smith goes on to argue that the primary importance of the Mass is the offering of the sacrifice, not the communion of the faithful, by saying that the commemoration is made:

"more chiefly, more lively and expressly by offering of the very Body and Blood in sacrifice, which is done by the priest in his Mass than by eating."

In fact, as Dom Gregory Dix has pointed out, the primary purpose of attending Mass was to see the elevation of the host, not to make communion. The average medieval Catholic would make his communion only once a year and that only under pressure from the Church. It was also thought by many that the more Masses that were offered for a particular purpose, the more benefit there would be. Mass was seen to be a series of individual sacrifices rather than a representation of the one great Sacrifice of Christ. It is for this reason that the Articles of Religion speak of "Sacrifices of Masses" in Article XXXI as being condemned.

The English Reformers repudiated the medieval development of "Sacrifices of Masses" and also objected to the concept of a propitiatory sacrifice insofar as the term implies a placating of God. Thomas Cranmer, Archbishop of Canterbury, in his reply to Stephen Gardiner, shows that there are two different views of sacrifice in the Eucharist:

> "One kind of sacrifice there is, which is called propitiatory or merciful sacrifice, that is to say, such a sacrifice as pacifieth God's wrath and indignation, and obtaineth mercy and forgiveness for all our sins, and is the ransom for our redemption from everlasting damnation...
>
> "Another kind of sacrifice there is which doth not reconcile us to God, but is made of them that be reconciled by Christ, to testify our duties unto God, and to show ourselves thankful unto Him. And therefore they be called sacrifices of laud, praise, and thanksgiving."

Cranmer pointed up the difference between the Romanists on the one hand and the Anglican reformers on the other:

> "The controversy is not whether in the Holy Communion be made a sacrifice or not (for herein both Dr. Smith and I agree with the foresaid Council at Ephesus), but whether it be a propitiatory sacrifice or not, and whether only the priest make the said sacrifice — these be the points wherein we vary."

Cranmer asserted that he believed in a sacrifice in the Eucharist, commonly called a Eucharist Sacrifice, but simply denies the propitiatory concept:

> "(Dr. Smith) belieth me by saying ... that I deny the sacrifice of the Mass, which in my book hath most plainly set out the sacrifice of the Christian people in the Holy Communion or Mass (if Dr. Smith will need so term it); and yet I have denied that it is a sacrifice propitiatory for sin, or that the priest alone maketh sacrifice there."

Another Reformer who held ideas similar to Cranmer was Nicholas Ridley. In 1548, he had written:

> "The representation and commemoration of Christ's death and passion, said and done in the Mass, is called the sacrifice of the Mass:

In 1555, on trial for his life, Ridley further stated, concerning the sacrifice of the Mass:

> "(F)or the Sacrament of the lively sacrifice (after which sort we denieth not to be in the Lord's Supper) ... our unbloody sacrifice of the Church (is) the sacrifice of praise and thanksgiving, ... a commemoration, a showing forth, and a sacramental representation of that one only bloody sacrifice, offered up once for all."

At the trial, Ridley was asked, "What say you to that council, where it is said, that the priest doth offer an unbloody sacrifice of the Body of Christ?" He replied:

> "I say, it is well said, if it be rightly understood ... It is called unbloody, and is offered after a certain manner, and in a mystery, and as a representation of that bloody sacrifice; and he doth not lie who sayeth Christ be offered."

Thomas Cranmer had also written concerning the nature of the sacrifice:

> "(B)ecause we daily sin, we daily be put in the remembrance of Christ's death, which is the perfect propitiation for sin ... and this is the priest's and people's sac-

rifice ... and this shortly is the mind of Lombardus, that the thing which is done at God's board is a sacrifice, and so is that also which was made upon the cross ... Petrus Lombardus defaceth in no point my saying of the sacrifice, but confirmeth fully my doctrine ... "

Here, then, was the point of difference between Anglican Reformers and the pro-Romanists.

The second question concerning the Real Presence is much more complex. It concerns whether the Body and Blood of Christ be present in the outward signs of the Eucharist, that is, the bread and wine. Both sides to the controversy clearly teach that Christ is present in the Eucharist but the *way* in which he is present is a source of great difference. Cranmer, himself, appeared to have rejected the concept of a Real Objective Presence. That is to say, he denied that Christ was truly present in the Eucharist but was at most present only in a "spiritual" manner. It was for this reason that the so-called Black Rubric was inserted in the 1552 Prayer Book, denying any "real and essential presence."

Cranmer said;

"I teach that no man can eat Christ's flesh and drink his blood but spiritually, which for as much as evil men do not, although they eat the sacramental bread until their bellies be full and drink the wine until they be drunken, yet they eat neither Christ's flesh nor drink His blood, neither in the Sacrament nor without the Sacrament, because they cannot be eaten and drunken but by spirit and flesh, whereof Godly men be destitute, being nothing but world and flesh."

"My doctrine is that the very Body of Christ, which was born of the Virgin Mary and suffered for our sins, giving us life by His death, the same Jesus, as concerning His corporal presence, taken from us and sitteth at the right hand of his father ... "*

Thus, Cranmer taught that there was no *Real* Presence in the Eucharist. In fact, he was the apparent author of the in-

---

*(Quotations from Gardiner, Smith, Cranmer and Ridley are taken from John J. Hughes, *Stewards of the Lord,* and Phillip E. Hughes, *Theology of the English Reformers.)*

famous "Black Rubric" referred to, which was added to the Second Prayer Book without authority of the Church. That rubric states in part:

> "We do declare that it is not meant thereby, that any adoration is done, or ought to be done, either unto the Sacramental bread or wine there bodily received, or unto any real and essential presence there being of Christ's natural flesh and blood. For ... as concerning the natural body and blood of our saviour Christ, they are in heaven and not here; for it is against the truth of Christ's true natural body, to be in more places than in one at one time."

Cranmer denied any belief in an Objective Real Presence of Our Lord in the Eucharist for the reason that he believed Christ took his natural body with him when he ascended into heaven, is currently present in heaven, and if he is seated at the right hand of the Father in heaven as the Creeds state, then he cannot be present in the Eucharist. A body can only be one place at a time. To Cranmer the Heavenly Presence ruled out any Objective Eucharistic Real Presence. In this Cranmer approached the theology of Ulrich Zwingli, a sixteenth century Protestant reformer. However, the Church does not, and in spite of Cranmer's efforts, never did, accept what Cranmer tried to force on it in the Black Rubric.

The doctrine of Eucharistic Sacrifice, clearly taught by the Church, is directly related to the doctrine of the Real Presence. As the great Tractarian, Edward. B. Pusey, wrote: "The doctrine of the Eucharistic Sacrifice depends upon the doctrine of the real objective presence."

The Standing Liturgical Commission of the Episcopal Church said in *Prayer Book Studies IV*, commenting on Cranmer and Zwingli: "The essential defect of their position lay in their consequently discarding the conception of an Objective Real Presence as useless — whereas actually *it is indispensable* (emphasis added)," as Dr. Pusey noted.

Cranmer's problem lay with the term "Body of Christ." He constantly identified it with Our Lord's *natural* body. However, he never saw that the term "Body of Christ" referred to a number of things, not just the natural body of Jesus of Nazareth.

THE EUCHARIST

The acceptable teaching of the Anglican Church is set forth in *Doctrine in the Church of England*, the Report of the Commission of Christian Doctrine, appointed by the Archbishops of Canterbury and York in 1922. The report states:

> "(a) In the New Testament a number of things are called Christ's Body: (1) the natural body in which He lived His earthly life and died upon the Cross; (2) the glorified body of His risen and ascended life; (3) His mystical body, the Church; (4) His Eucharistic body.
>
> (b) That which is common to all of these is that each is in some sense an embodiment of our Lord – ie., a means through which the life of the Incarnate is made accessible to man.
>
> (c) The language of I Cor. x. 17 suggests some kind of interconnexion between the Eucharistic body and the mystical body. ('the bread which we break, is it not a communion of the body of Christ? For we, being many, are one bread, one body; for we all partake of the one bread.')
>
> (d) On the other hand, the Eucharistic body is differentiated from the mystical body by the fact that in the Eucharist the Body and the Blood are so closely associated with one another."

Thus, the Standing Liturgical Commission could put its finger directly on the failure of Cranmer:

> "The Church's teaching has always been that at the Ascension our Lord's Body, as the vehicle of his Humanity, was *glorified*, raised to the spiritual level, and universalized above all local limitations: so that the Incarnate Lord is now everywhere present in his Humanity as well as his Divinity. It is not the Natural Body which is physically, materially, naturally, spatially, and locally present in the Holy Eucharist, but the Glorified Body, present metaphysically, immaterially, supernaturally, extra-spatially, and supra-locally, after the manner of a spirit (Prayer Book Studies IV)."

The commission went on to state that the Church never accepted the Zwinglian concepts of Cranmer and that even

Cranmer was unable, through the Black Rubric or his liturgy, to push the Church into heresy:

> "In other words, Cranmer's personal opinions were certainly theologically defective, and may be conceded to have been heretical. But in spite of all he could do, his liturgy was not heretical, even in the impoverished form of the Second Prayer Book."

Finally, the attempt of Cranmer to impose his Zwinglian view upon the Church failed inasmuch as the Black Rubric in the 1552 Prayer Book was submitted and incorporated without authority of the Church and was removed from the 1559 Prayer Book and reinserted in the 1662 Prayer Book, but with a change in language from denying a "real and essential presence" to "corporal presence." In other words, the Church denies transubstantiation in its claim of a *corporal* presence of Christ but does not deny that he *is* really present.

We may therefore sum up the broad position of the Anglican Reformers to be that the Eucharist is a Sacrifice, although not a new sacrifice of Christ in each celebration, and that Christ is really present in the Eucharist, but not corporally so. This viewpoint of Sacrifice and Real Presence is clearly taught today. As the Prayer Book says of Eucharistic Sacrifice in the Catechism:

> "Q. Why is the Eucharist called a sacrifice?
>
> A. Because it is the Church's sacrifice of praise and thanksgiving, by which Christ unites us to his one offering of himself."

And as General Convention said of the Real Presence at Denver in 1979:

> "The positive response to the Anglican-Roman International Commission's Agreed Statement on the Eucharist (Windsor 1971) undergirds the strong agreement in this Church and the recognition of *Christ's real presence in this sacrament* (emphasis added)."

Having declared this, Convention then stated five preconditions to receiving communion in the Episcopal Church. The third of these is:

"They shall approach the Holy Communion as an *expression of the Real Presence of Jesus Christ* whose sacrifice once upon the cross was sufficient for all mankind (emphasis added)."

Indeed, the current thrust of Anglican Eucharistic development is such that a recent Roman Catholic author, Edward P. Echlin, a Jesuit, writing in *The Anglican Eucharist in Ecumenical Perspective*, was able to say:

"In the study we have just concluded, we examined the historic development of Anglican Eucharistic doctrine during three centuries and on two continents. We have found that from the Reformation to recent times, Anglican doctrine has tended to converge with that of the Roman Catholic Church. The conclusion we have reached from a historical point of view concurs with that of a recent commission of Anglicans and Roman Catholics who have been studying contemporary doctrinal formulations on Eucharistic sacrifice, theologians and bishops of both churches said: 'Since the time of the Reformation, the doctrine of Eucharistic sacrifice has been considered a major obstacle to the reconciliation of the Anglican Communion and the Roman Catholic Church. It is the conviction of our commission that this is no longer true.'

"In our historic study we have also found that since the Elizabethan settlement, comprehensiveness has been a component of Anglican services. The rite of the Episcopal Church is as susceptible as the Roman Mass to interpretation in terms of propitiatory sacrifice and perduring real presence. In fact, there is one component of the Episcopal Canon – the invocation insisted on by Seabury – that possibly teaches real presence more explicitly than the Roman Mass."

Finally, one can honestly say that the whole Anglican Communion, in the process of liturgical reform, liturgical study and Biblical examination is making full use of scholarship to maintain the Scriptural truth and ancient shape of the liturgy. In the process it is breaking down the barriers of separation erected by the misunderstanding and misdirection created by the narrow, polemic views of the middle ages.

CHAPTER 6

Other Sacramental Rites

PENANCE

"Q. What is Reconciliation of a Penitent?

"A. Reconciliation of a Penitent, or Penance, is the rite in which those who repent of their sins may confess them to God in the presence of a priest, and receive the assurance of pardon and the grace of absolution (Prayer Book, p. 861)."

The sacramental rite of Penance, like Confirmation, is not a rite to which Our Lord gave a specific form or matter. However, it arose as a necessary corollary to the washing away of sins in Baptism. We are told that Baptism does remit sins (e.g. Acts ii. 38; Acts xxii. 16). However, sin may be committed after Baptism and a baptized Christian can fall from grace (Gal. v. 4). If we do fall from grace after Baptism may our sins be forgiven? In answering this question we must remember that in the Old Testament the sign of the forgiveness of sins was the sprinkling of the people of Israel with the blood of sacrifice (e.g. Exodus). The sacrificial system of the Old Testament provided for sin offerings.

In the New Testament, the price of our sins is paid in the sacrifice of Our Lord on the Cross. As St. John said:

"If any man sin, we have an advocate with the Father, Jesus Christ the righteous; and he is the perfect offering (expiation) for our sins, and not for ours only, but for the sins of the whole world (I Jn. ii. 1-2)."

Many of St. Paul's admonitions to sinful Christians bear witness to their having fallen from grace; and the fact they once had grace and that it is restored after repentance is clearly implied. (Acts viii. 13, 8-23; I Cor. iii. 16, 17; vi. 11-20; ix. 26, 27; Gal. v. 2, 4, 19-21). However, forgiveness of sins requires a confession of them on our part, which implies repentance. Penance is generally said to consist of three parts – contrition, confession and satisfaction. Preceeding these is self-examination and following upon them is the work of amendment. As St. John said (I Jn. i. 9), "If we confess our sins, he is faithful and just to forgive us our sins."

Self-examination is very important, especially as we approach the Eucharist. St. Paul warned the Corinthian Christians of this fact when he said (I Cor. xi. 28), "But let a man examine himself." St. James said in his Epistle General (v. 16), "Therefore confess your sins to one another, and pray for one another, and then you will be healed."

The authority to pronounce the absolution and forgiveness which Our Lord purchased by his death on the cross was given by him to his apostles:

> "Receive the Holy Spirit. If you forgive any man his sins, they stand forgiven; if you pronounce them unforgiven, unforgiven they remain (Jn. xx. 22-23)."

This authority to pronounce absolution was not only possessed by the apostles, but apparently was exercised by the elders (priests), as well (James v. 14, 15). Thus, while our sins are washed away in Baptism, we may fall from grace and commit sins thereafter. However, God provides a means of forgiving us of those sins if we but repent and confess our sins, amending our lives and receiving absolution from the bishop or priest acting with the authority given them by Christ.

HOLY MATRIMONY

"Q. What is Holy Matrimony?

"A. Holy Matrimony is Christian Marriage, in which the woman and man enter into a life-long union, make their vows before God and the Church, and receive the grace and blessing of God to help them fulfill their vows (Prayer Book, p. 861)."

Holy Matrimony is a sacramental rite representing an indissoluble or lifelong union between man and woman that "signifies to us the mystery of the union between Christ and his Church."

Marriage is a civil contract and has always thus been recognized by various societies and governments. However, it is more; it is a sacred relationship. As Christians, we must therefore look to the teaching of Our Lord. St. Mark records the following discourse on marriage and divorce in chapter 10 of his Gospel:

> "The question was put to him: 'Is it lawful for a man to divorce his wife?' This was to test him. He asked in return, 'What did Moses command you?' They answered, 'Moses permitted a man to divorce his wife by note of dismissal.' Jesus said to them, 'It was because your minds were closed that he made this rule for you; but in the beginning, at the creation, God made them male and female. For this reason a man shall leave his father and mother, and be made one with his wife; and the two shall become one flesh. It follows that they are no longer two individuals: They are one flesh. What God has joined together, man must not separate.'"

When Our Lord's Apostles questioned him about this, he said, "Whoever divorces his wife and marries another commits adultery against her: So too, if she divorces her husband and marries another, she commits adultery." St. Luke also records the same teaching (Lk. xvi. 18):

> "A man who divorces his wife and marries another commits adultery; and anyone who marries a woman divorced from her husband commits adultery."

St. Matthew, with one notable exception, records the same teaching:

> "They were told, 'A man who divorces his wife must give her a note of dismissal.' But what I tell you is this: If a man divorces his wife for any cause other than unchastity he involves her in adultery; and anyone who marries a divorced woman commits adultery (Matt. v. 32, 33)."

Again, St. Matthew states:

"Some Pharisees came and tested him by asking, 'Is it lawful for a man to divorce his wife on any and every ground?' He asked in return, 'Have you never read that the creator made them from the beginning male and female?'; and he added, 'For this reason a man shall leave his father and mother, and be made one with his wife; and the two shall become one flesh. It follows that they are no longer two individuals; they are one flesh. What God has joined together, man must not separate.' 'Why then', they objected, 'did Moses lay it down that a man might divorce his wife by a note of dismissal?' He answered, "It was because your minds were closed that Moses gave you permission to divorce you wives; but it was not like that when all began. I tell you, if a man divorces his wife for any cause other than unchastity, and marries another, he commits adultery' (Matt. xix. 3-9)."

The exception noted in Matthew is the apparent ground for the commission of adultery as allowing divorce and remarriage. Since all other passages quoting Our Lord do not grant this exception, it is argued that either (1) the clause "except for unchastity" was later inserted into the text; (2) that Our Lord would allow the innocent party of an adultery to divorce and remarry; or in the final alternative, (3) the clause may simply refer to the permission for separation, confirming what Our Lord had said in Matthew v. 32. The remarriage of the husband, whatever the cause of separation, would then be declared to be adultery, just as it is by Mark and Luke.

St. Paul indicates also the indissoluble nature of marriage as he wrote at the beginning of chapter 7 of his Epistle to the Church at Rome:

"You cannot be unaware, my friends – I am speaking to those who have some knowledge of the law – that a person is subject to the law so long as he is alive, and no longer. For example, a married women is by law bound to her husband while he lives; but if her husband dies, she is discharged from the obligations of the marriage law. If, therefore, in her husband's lifetime she consorts with another man, she will incur the charge of adultery; but if her husband dies she is free of the law, and she does not commit adultery by consorting with another man."

Again, Paul says in his first Epistle to the Corinthians (vii. 10, 11):

"To the married I give this ruling, which is not mine but the Lord's: A wife must not separate herself from her husband; if she does, she must either remain unmarried or be reconciled to her husband; and the husband must not divorce his wife."

Paul indicates, however, that the rule is not quite the same if one of the parties is not Christian (I Cor. vii. 12-16).

Finally, St. Paul presents a moving passage reflecting the nature of Christian marriage:

"Be subject to one another out of reverence for Christ.

"Wives, be subject to your husbands as to the Lord; for the man is the head of the woman, just as Christ also is the head of the Church. Christ is, indeed, the saviour of the body; but just as the Church is subject to Christ, so must women be to their husbands in everything.

"Husbands, love your wives, as Christ also loved the Church and gave himself up for it, to consecrate it, cleansing it by water and word, so that he might present the Church to himself all glorious, with no stain or wrinkle or anything of the sort, but holy and without blemish. In the same way men also are bound to love their wives, as they love their own bodies. In loving his wife a man loves himself. For no one ever hated his own body: On the contrary, he provides for it and cares for it; and that is how Christ treats the Church, because it is his body, of which we are living parts. Thus it is that (in the words of Scripture) 'A man shall leave his father and mother and shall be joined to his wife, and the two shall become one flesh.'

"It is a great truth that is hidden here. I for my part refer it to Christ and to the Church, but it applies also individually: Each of you must love his wife as his very self; and the woman must see to it that she pays her husband all respect (Eph. v. 21-33)."

HOLY UNCTION

"Q. What is Unction of the Sick?

"A. Unction is the rite of anointing the sick with oil, or the laying on of hands, by which God's grace is given for the healing of spirit, mind, and body (Prayer Book, p. 861)."

Our Lord was greatly concerned with human illness and the Gospels are filled with many accounts of his healing grace. We are told that he restored sight to the blind, that he cleansed lepers, that he gave speech and hearing to the deaf and dumb, that he caused the crippled to walk, and even when the people had no faith in him and his miracles were few, he did heal the sick.

During his earthly ministry, Our Lord directed the apostles to heal, even as he did. St. Mark tells us that he sent the twelve out in pairs on a mission, and "They drove out many devils, and many sick people they anointed with oil and cured (Mk. vi. 13)." St. Paul tells us that the gift of healing is the operation of the Holy Spirit (I Cor. xii. 9). The Church has traditionally looked to the example as cited by St. James, in chapter 5 of his Epistle General, as the norm of sacramental Unction:

"Is one of you ill? He should send for the elders of the congregation to pray over him and anoint him with oil in the name of the Lord. The prayer offered in faith will save the sick man, the Lord will raise him from his bed, and any sins he may have committed will be forgiven."

Unction is referred to in the same familiar terms as prayer and the use of the Psalter in the preceding verse of James' Epistle and it is taken for granted that the elders of the Church expect to be summoned to the sick for the administering of this sacramental rite.

While Scripture does not point to any example of Our Lord's specifically instituting this sacrament, the above quoted passage from St. Mark's Gospel indicates that, in a sense at least, the sacrament was foreshadowed by Our Lord. The Orthodox Church cites this passage in its official formularies as the account of the occasion upon which Christ himself ordained it.

By tradition, therefore, oil is seen as the matter of Unction. However, the Episcopal Church in the United States recognizes both anointing with oil and laying on of hands. The use of the laying on of hands is based upon examples of healing in the New Testament by such a means (e.g. Acts iv. 30: "Stretch out thy hand to heal," in the prayer of supplication to God: And the specific statement in Mark's Gospel, xvi. 18: "And the sick on whom they lay their hands will recover"). Whether by laying on of hands or by anointing with oil, the Church has ever exercised the ministry of Our Lord in healing the sick.

PART IV

The Ministry

The same section of the Prayer Book which we cited in regard to the other sacramental rites of the Church (Catechism, page 861), also speaks of the ordained ministry, and Ordination:

> "Ordination is the rite in which God gives authority and the grace of the Holy Spirit to those being made bishops, priests and deacons, through prayer and and the laying on of hands by bishops."

In the Preface to the Ordination Rites, the Prayer Book says:

> "The Holy Scriptures and ancient Christian writers make it clear that from the apostles' time, there have been different ministries within the Church. In particular, since the time of the New Testament, three distinct orders of ordained ministers have been characteristic of Christ's holy catholic Church. First, there is the order of bishops who carry on the apostolic work of leading, supervising, and uniting the Church. Secondly, associated with them are the presbyters, or ordained elders, in subsequent times generally known as priests. Together with the bishops, they take part in the governance of the Church, in the carrying out of its missionary and pastoral work, and in the preaching of the Word of God and administering his holy Sacraments. Thirdly, there are deacons who assist bishops and priests in all of this work. It is also a special responsibility of deacons to minister in Christ's name to the poor, the sick, the suffering, and the helpless.

"The persons who are chosen and recognized by the Church as being called by God to the ordained ministry are admitted to these sacred orders by solemn prayer and the laying on of episcopal hands. It has been, and is, the intention and purpose of this Church to maintain and continue these three orders; and for this purpose these services of ordination and consecration are appointed. No persons are allowed to exercise the offices of bishop, priest, or deacon in this Church unless they are so ordained, or have already received such ordination with the laying on of hands by bishops who are themselves duly qualified to confer Holy Orders.

"It is also recognized and affirmed that the threefold ministry is not the exclusive property of this portion of Christ's catholic Church, but is a gift from God for the nurture of His people and the proclamation of His Gospel everywhere. Accordingly, the manner of ordaining in this Church is to be such as has been, and is, most generally recognized by Christian people as suitable for the conferring of the sacred orders of bishop, priest, and deacon (Prayer Book, p. 510)."

Chapter 7 will review the Scriptural and historical basis for this threefold ministry of Apostolic Succession.

CHAPTER 7

The Threefold Ministry of Apostolic Succession

"It is evident unto all men, diligently reading Holy Scripture and ancient authors, that from the Apostles' time there have been these Orders of Ministers in Christ's Church, – Bishops, Priests and Deacons."

These words, from the *Preface to the Ordinal* in the First Book of Common Prayer, affirm the belief of the Church that a certain form of ministry has always existed "from the Apostles' time." These ministers are "Ministers of Apostolic Succession," as the Office of Institution of the earlier Prayer Book says. What is "Apostolic Succession" and is Apostolic Succession "evident . . . (from) Holy Scripture and ancient Authors"? This is our primary task; to examine the writings of the Church Fathers and Holy Writ, to see what kind of Church Order existed and if that form of Order now exists in the Church.

Apostolic Succession is the doctrine of a ministry in unbroken succession from the Apostles. According to this doctrine, the Twelve Apostles, ordained by Our Lord, ordained successors to their office and authority and these successors ordained other men to take their place and so on continuing to the present day. These successors to the apostles are the bishops of the Church.

The book, *Apostle in Our Midst*, by David B. Joslin, has been used by the House of Bishops of the Episcopal Church to understand the nature of the episcopate in our age. In that book Joslin points out that Anglicans hold three different positions in regard to the nature of the episcopate: *bene esse, esse,* and *plene esse* (pp. 36-41). *Bene esse* means that the episcopate of Apostolic Succession is of the well being of the

Church but is not essential in any way; it is only a good system of Church polity. *Esse* holds that the Apostolic Succession is essential to the Church and that the ministry and sacraments depend upon it. *Plene esse* states that the episcopate is of the fullness of the Church and that while a Christian community may be a Church without the episcopate, only those churches which possess the Apostolic Succession are fully Churches.

From this it can be seen that Anglicans permit some variety of belief in regard to the ministry. However, while differences of theological positions are permitted, we must make a distinction between the area of permissible theological belief and the pragmatic law of what the Church in her daily life actually requires. Basically, the requirement of Church law is that whether one believes in *bene esse, esse,* or *plene esse,* the Church nonetheless will require a ministry of the episcopate in Apostolic Succession. In other words, while one is allowed to hold, in theory, either the *bene esse* or *plene esse* principle, the practice of the Church as reflected in official statements and canon law tends to adhere to the *esse* theory. The reason for this is the importance of the doctrine of Apostolic Succession as a principle "incapable of compromise or surrender" and "therefore as essential to the restoration of unity," to quote the Chicago Quadrilaterial.

The importance of the doctrine of Apostolic Succession can be seen if we think of the Church as a Sacramental Society, receiving God's Grace through the channels of the Sacraments. We receive the Sacrament of the Body and Blood of Our Lord, for example, from the priest and a priest must be ordained by the bishop. The bishop must have been ordained by other bishops and those bishops likewise ordained, and so continuing back in an unbroken line to the Twelve Apostles and Our Lord. If the bishop is not in this line of Apostolic Succession he does not have the authority to ordain priests and without priests there is no Eucharistic Sacrament and no Sacramental Society. As it was stated in the English Civil War of the seventeenth century, "No Bishop, no Church." The Bishop and Apostolic Succession, then may be said to be necessary if the Church is to receive the fullness of the Grace of God.

Implicit in the doctrine of Apostolic Succession is the idea of a threefold ministry of bishops, priests and deacons. At times these various orders may be called by different names, but three distinct orders can at all times be discerned. Another idea implicit in Apostolic Succession is the idea of episcopacy. The unity and authority of the Church center around the episcopate as the source of continuity of Orders. The unity and authority of the episcopate are part of the peculiar ethos of Anglicanism and the Anglican Communion has been distinguished by an episcopal form of Church polity. These are the things we shall look for in our study of Apostolic Succession: a ministry in unbroken succession from the apostles, a threefold form to that ministry, and an episcopate as a focal point of the ministry.

At a time when there is so much talk of Christian Reunion, it is important to know what the Church believes and what elements of the Anglican ethos must be preserved in any Church Union. We must see if there is a particular concept of the ministry that should be considered essential to the faith. If so, it should be preserved at all costs.

Let us look, first, at the Biblical basis for the ordained ministry. When we examine Holy Scripture, we find that God established a Holy Ministry long before the established Christian Era. This Priesthood of God was to exist forever and was a type or shadow of the coming priesthood of the new Dispensation of Our Lord in which the Holy Priesthood finds its continuity and means of succession. In Exodus xi. 15, the priesthood is said to "be an everlasting priesthood throughout (all) generations." This idea of an everlasting priesthood is mentioned again as "the covenant of an everlasting priesthood (Num. xxv. 14)." Thus, we see that God intends for his priesthood to exist forever.

This Old Testament ministry is a threefold one. We can easily distinguish the order of high priest, priests and levites throughout the Jewish Dispensation. For example, we read of the Consecration of Aaron as high priest in the Book of Exodus (Ex. xxix. 5-7), "And thou shalt take the garments, and put upon Aaron the coat, and the robe of the ephod, and the ephod, and the breastplate, and gird him with the curious girdle of the ephod; and thou shalt put the mitre upon his head, and put the holy crown upon the mitre. Then shalt thou take the anointing oil, and pour it upon his head, and anoint him."

Also, we read that priests are consecrated or ordered to serve with the high priest (Ex. xxviii. 40, 41):

"And for Aaron's sons thou shalt make coats, and thou shalt make for them girdles, and bonnets shalt thou make for them, for glory and for beauty. And thou shalt put them upon (Aaron's) sons; and shalt anoint them, and consecrate them, and sanctify them, that they may minister unto me in the priest's office."

The third order of the Jewish Priesthood was the levites. Their purpose was to serve the high priest and priests and "do the service of the tabernacle" as we read in the Book of Numbers (Num. iii. 6-10):

"Bring the tribe of Levi near, and present them before Aaron the priest, that they may minister unto him. And they shall keep his charge, and the charge of the whole congregation before the tabernacle of the congregation, to do the service of the tabernacle. And they shall keep all the instruments of the tabernacle of the congregation, and the charge of the children of Israel, to do the service of the tabernacle. And thou shalt give the Levites unto Aaron and to his sons; they are wholly given unto him out of the children of Israel. And thou shalt appoint Aaron and his sons, and they shall wait on their priest's office; and the stranger that cometh nigh shall be put to death."

We have, then, a threefold ministry of high priest, priest and levite. And there was a succession in this priesthood. For example, we read that Eleazar succeeds Aaron in the office of high priest upon Aaron's death. "Strip Aaron of his garments, and put them upon Eleazar his son: And Aaron shall be gathered unto his people, and shall die there (Num. xx. 26)." Later, Eleazar is succeeded by Phinehas (Num. xxv. 11). So we can see a priestly succession in operation.

When Our Lord came, he did not destroy the law or the priesthood, but brought them to fulfillment. This allowed the continuity of the priesthood as everlasting and explains Our Lord's words when he said (Matt. v. 17), "Think not that I am come to destroy the law or the prophets; I am come not to destroy, but to fulfil."

The early Christian Church built upon this foundation of the Jewish community, especially in its form of the ministry. We can see certain similarities in a threefold ministry and a line of succession. Thus, God's promise that the ministry will be an "everlasting priesthood" is fulfilled as this priesthood is continued in Christianity.

As Our Lord began his ministry, he called to him twelve who were to be the apostles. These twelve were ordained and made apostles by Our Lord, himself. We read in St. Mark's Gospel (Mk. iii. 14), "And he ordained twelve, that they should be with him, and that he might send them forth . . . " We read similar accounts in Matt. 1. The apostles, then, were so ordained by Christ. Now these apostles were mainly responsible for the form of the Christian Church. They were given authority and ordained by God the Son and they were responsible for the spread of the Church. Their Holy Office was to be eternal and remain with the Church forever. "Lo, I (Christ) am with you (Apostolate) alway, even unto the end of the world (Matt. xxviii. 20)."

The Apostolate, then, is to be with Christ forever and we see that this Apostolate is to be guided by the Holy Ghost the Comforter, the Spirit of Truth – forever. "And I will pray the Father, and he shall give you another Comforter, that he may abide with you forever; even the Spirit of truth (Jn. xiv. 16, 17)." This Church Order (the Apostolate) is to be preserved by the presence of Jesus Christ and the Holy Ghost. Thus preserved, this Apostolic Order is to be guided into all truth (John xvi. 13). "Howbeit when he, the Spirit of truth, is come, he will guide you into all truth." The Church of Christ, then, possesses the Apostolic Order which is guided into all truth. Thus fortified, the Church shall never be destroyed. "Upon this rock I will build my church; and the gates of hell shall not prevail against it (Matt. xvi. 18)."

If the Apostolate of the Church is to be continued, there must be a succession of "other men" to replace those that die and to spread the work of the Church. After all, it is God's intent that this be an "everlasting priesthood" and Christ promised that even "the gates of hell shall not prevail against it." The Apostles have the power to ordain others as Christ ordained them. This we see in Acts i. 22, where the Apostles have the power – the obligation – to ordain men to the Apostolate. The first such ordination is that of Matthias, who is ordained to succeed Judas Iscariot, "That he may take part of this ministry and apostleship, from which Judas by transgression fell, that he might go to his own place (Acts i. 25)." Later, men like St. Paul are ordained Apostles. "Whereunto I (Paul) am ordained a preacher, and an apostle, (I speak the truth in Christ and lie not;) a teacher of the Gentiles in faith and verity (I Tim. ii. 7)." We see, then, a succession of ministry; an *Apostolic Succession.*

In addition to the Apostolate, there are other Orders of the Ministry. The first Order to be established was the Order of Deacons (from *diakonos,* Greek for servant). This order was to serve the Church in works of charity, caring for widows and others (Acts vi. 1). Seven deacons were chosen and ordained by the apostles. "They chose Stephen, a man full of faith and of the Holy Ghost, and Philip, and Prochorus, and Nicanor, and Timon, and Parmenas, and Nicolas a proselyte of Antioch: Whom they set before the apostles: And when they had prayed, they laid their hands on them (Acts vi. 5, 6)." St. Paul says of deacons (I Tim. iii. 8-10), "Likewise must the deacons be grave, not double-tongued, not given to much wine, not greedy of filthy lucre; holding the mystery of the faith in a pure conscience. And let these also first be proved; then let them use the office of a deacon, being found blameless." The Order of Deacon corresponds to the levites; both orders serve in the Church; both orders are the third rank of the ministry.

A second Order of Ministers was then created, the Order of Elders, presbyters, or priests (from *presbyteros,* Greek for Elder).

"And when they had ordained them elders in every church, and had prayed with fasting, they commended them to the Lord, on whom they believed (Acts xiv. 23)."

Another term was sometimes used for this second order – the term "bishop" (from *episkopos,* Greek for overseer). In Titus i. 5, St. Paul refers to this order as elders ("ordain elders"), but in Titus i. 7 he calls these elders "bishops" ("a bishop must be blameless"). However, the term "bishop" applies also to the apostolic office, as we can see in Acts i. 20 when Matthias succeeds to the bishoprick *(episkopen)* of Judas.

We can see a threefold ministry developing in the New Testament: apostle, elder and deacon. We can see a clear example of this threefold ministry when Paul and Timothy, men of the apostolic *episkopē,* address the elders and deacons of Philippi, together with the faithful souls, the saints. "Paul and Timotheus, the servants of Jesus Christ, to all the saints in

Christ Jesus which are at Philippi, with the bishops (elders) and deacons (Phil. i. 1)." Here we have apostles, bishops and deacons; a threefold ministry such as had been under the Jewish Dispensation; "the covenant of an everlasting priesthood."

This Timothy, who was with Paul and shared in the Apostolic *episkopē*, was ordained to his office by Paul and succeeded Paul in the work of the Church at Ephesus:

> "Wherefore I put thee in remembrance that thou stir up the gift of God, which is in thee by the putting on of my hands (II Tim. i. 6)."

We read in the Acts of the Apostles that Paul exercised authority over the Church at Ephesus and taught and preached among the Elders (Acts xx. 17-26). After Paul left Ephesus, he placed Timothy in charge (I Tim. x. 3). Timothy (who was ordained by Paul) was Paul's equal and brother in Christ (Phil, i. 1; Colos. i. 1, Cor. i. 1). Timothy did the work of God in the manner and authority of Paul (I Cor. xvi. 10). At Ephesus Timothy was to oversee (have authority over) the elders (I Tim. v. 17); he was also to judge them (I Tim. v. 19); and finally, he had authority to ordain to the Holy Ministry (I Tim. v. 22).

As Timothy carried out the apostolic work at Ephesus, so also did Titus at Crete. St. Paul had put Titus in charge of the churches at Crete (Titus i. 5): "For this cause left I thee in Crete, that thou shouldest set in order the things that are wanting . . ." As Timothy had authority over the churches at Ephesus and ordained (I Tim. v. 22), and as the apostles had ordained elders in the churches (Acts xiv. 23), so Titus also ordained elders in the cities of Crete (Titus i. 5). "Thou shouldest . . . ordain elders in every city, as I had appointed thee." It is evident in Holy Scripture, then, that the Apostolic Office was continued.

The idea of one man holding the apostolic *episkopē* over the local groupings of churches emerges as the Church develops. First, we saw that the apostles were ordained by Christ (Mark iii. 14); the apostles had the power to ordain succeeding apostles (Acts i. 22), and they did so. For example, Matthias was ordained by the apostles to succeed Judas Iscariot (Acts i. 25, 26).

At first, these apostles were in charge of all the churches, ordaining elders (Acts xiv. 23) and deacons (Acts vi. 6) in the churches. Later, one man holding the apostolic authority would be set over churches in designated areas as Timothy was placed in charge of the churches in Ephesus (I Tim. i. 3), and Titus in Crete (Titus i. 5). That this form of organization was to continue we can see from the Revelation in St. John the Divine. In the Book of Revelation we read especially of the Seven Churches of Asia that are governed by a single minister call an angel. The first mentioned is the angel of Ephesus, such as Timothy, who had charge of the Church of Ephesus (Rev. ii. 1). Also mentioned is the Church of Smyrna (Rev. ii. 8), where Polycarp, the disciple of St. John, was Bishop at the time the passage was written (c. A.D. 100). In each of the other Churches (Pergamos, Thyatira, Sardis, Philadelphia, and Laodicea) there was a single man exercising the apostolic *episkopē* (Rev. ii. and iii.).

In brief then, Holy Scripture shows us a threefold ministry corresponding to a threefold Jewish Ministry, with an Apostolic Succession similar to the Priestly Succession of the Old Dispensation. The third order of the ministry was the deacon, the equivalent of the levite. Next was the elder, sometimes called presbyter, sometimes called bishop, equal to the priest. The final (and first) order of minister was the apostle, sometimes called bishop, corresponding to the high priest.

The term "deacon" has always been used for the third order of minister (e.g. I Tim. iii. 8). Of the two terms for the second order, "presbyter" (Acts xvi. 23) came to be used almost exclusively. The term "bishop" used both for elders (Titus i. 7) and apostles (Acts i. 20), gradually came to be used more and more to refer to those of the Apostolic Office only, while "Apostle" (Acts i. 20; xv. 2) was applied usually only to the Apostles chosen by Our Lord as the *first* to hold that office. (For this reason St. Patrick, first Bishop of Ireland is called the *apostle* of the Irish as St. Boniface is called the *apostle* of Germany, that is, the first bishop of Germany.) These terms have been used over the centuries, then, to refer to the ministry of the Church: bishop, presbyter, deacon.

"It is evident unto all men, diligently reading Holy Scripture . . . , that from the Apostles' time there have been these Orders of Ministers in Christ's Church, — Bishops, Priests, and Deacons." These ministers were all *ordained* to their office (Mark iii. 14; Acts xiv. 23; Acts vi. 6). This ordination was by the laying on of hands of the Apostles. This is explicitly mentioned in Acts vi. 6, for example, when the first deacons were ordained by laying on of hands. Likewise, Timothy was ordained by Paul by the laying on of hands (II Tim. i. 6). Timothy, himself, was to ordain by laying hands on the men ordained (I Tim. v. 22). In all other ordinations mentioned in Holy Scripture, laying on of hands was implicit (e.g. Acts xiv. 23). The Greek term used was *cheirotoneo*, to ordain *by the laying on of hands*. (The term comes from the word *cheir*, hand.) So we see that the threefold ministry was ordained by the laying on of hands.

The function of ordaining is limited to the Apostles and their successors only (Acts i. 22; Acts vi. 6; Acts xiv. 23; II Tim. 1.6; I Tim. v. 22; Titus i. 5); there is no example of an elder or deacon ever ordaining.

Having seen what Scripture says, let us turn to "Ancient Authors" of the Church. The extant writings of the Early Fathers are few in number and scant in material. However, we do have a representative sampling of material that is even more explicit and complete on Church Order than is Holy Scripture. We shall briefly examine the writings of the Church Fathers over a period of four centuries, from A.D. 91 to c. A.D. 385. The earliest of these works were written before the last of the New Testament was written and while St. John the Apostle yet lived.

The first "Ancient Author" we meet is St. Clement, bishop of Rome, and friend of St. Paul. He wrote in his *Epistle to the Corinthians* about episcopacy (government by bishops) and Apostolic Succession. The date is A.D. 91, several years before St. John wrote the Book of Revelation.

> "The Apostles knew through Our Lord Jesus Christ that contentions would arise about the Episcopacy, its name, its nature, and its authority; and for this reason, being endued with perfect foreknowledge, they appointed certain persons, and handed down an order of succession, so that when they should depart, other approved men should take their office and ministry."

Here St. Clement, the contemporary of St. John, and the associate of St. Paul, tells us that the Apostles established an Order of Succession (Apostolic Succession) centered in the episcopate. Thus we see the idea of Apostolic Succession is firmly believed and practiced before the close of the Apostolic Age. In the same letter, Clement speaks of the threefold ministry of apostles, bishops (elders), and deacons (chapter xix), and equates them to the Jewish ministry:

> "For the chief-priest has his proper services; and to the priests then proper place is appointed; and to the Levites appertain their proper ministries: and the layman is confined within the bounds of what is commanded to laymen."

Some fifteen years later another Church Father, St. Ignatius, bishop of Antioch, reportedly the child whom Our Lord took up and set in the midst of the Apostles to teach them a needed lesson of humility, wrote to the Church of Smyrna about the authority of the bishop in the Church:

> "Wheresoever the Bishop shall appear, there let the people also be: As where Jesus Christ is, there is the Catholic Church *(To the Church of Smyrna)*."

In his *Epistle to Philadelphia,* St. Ignatius speaks of the unity of the priesthood with the bishop (written c. A.D. 105):

> "Your estimable Priesthood is harmoniously joined with the Bishop, as strings to a harp; and therefore by your concord and unison of love, Christ is chanted, and ye all become a choir, so that, being attuned together and receiving divine melody in oneness of mind, ye may sing with one voice through Christ to God."

Ignatius later wrote to the Church of Tralles. Here we read of the threefold ministry of bishops, priests and deacons; also the authority of the bishop:

> "It is necessary to do nothing without the Bishop, but to be subject also to the Priests, as to the Apostles of Christ our hope; and the Deacons, who are ministers of Christ's Mysteries, ought to be pleasing to all for they are not ministers of food and drink, but of the Church of God *(Epistle to the Church of Tralles)*."

In this same Epistle, Ignatius is even more explicit about recognizing the threefold ministry of Apostolic Succession:

THE THREEFOLD MINISTRY OF APOSTOLIC SUCCESSION 143

"He that does anything without Bishop, and Presbyters, and Deacons, is not pure in conscience." Here St. Ignatius sets forth concisely the same Order we found in Holy Scripture, when he says "Bishop, and Presbyters, and Deacons."

In the middle of the second century a simple Christian soul called Hermas wrote *The Shepherd,* an account of life in the Church at Rome during the second century. Hermas speaks of a threefold Order of Ministry such as earlier writers have mentioned. At Rome the bishop is the "angel" or ruler of the Church. Hermas referred to the bishops as "rulers of the Church and the occupants of the chief seats." Some of the early Roman ministers were still alive while others had died, but a threefold ministry still existed:

> "In (the Church) are ... Bishops and Teachers (i.e. Priests) and Deacons. (Of these) who exercised their office of Bishop and Teacher (Priest) and Deacon (at Rome) ... Some of them (are) already fallen asleep, and others still living."

Towards the end of the second century, in the year 178, the Bishop of Lyons, France, St. Irenaeus, wrote an Apologia of the Church, defending the orthodox faith from the attacks of heretics. Irenaeus spoke of apostolic doctrine and truth being dependent upon Apostolic Succession through the bishops:

> "The doctrine of the Apostles is true knowledge; and the ancient state of the Church, and the character of the body of Christ, is according to the succession of Bishops to whom, in every place, they delivered the Church *(Work against Heresies)."*

In this same work Irenaeus asserts that a list of Apostolic Succession can be made and that at his time there had been no break in the succession:

> "We can enumerate those whom the Apostles appointed Bishops in the Churches, and their successors, even to us.... In this order and by this succession that tradition in the Church which is from the Apostles, hath come uninterruptedly to us."

A stern, imposing figure stands at the beginning of the third century of Christian experience — the learned priest and theologian, Tertullian. Tertullian was a strict, zealous Christian whose relentless drive finally led him into heterodox belief in his old age. Against those who reject apostolic tradition, Tertullian scorns to consider Scripture, since Scripture belongs to, and is interpreted by the true Church. This true Church Tertullian finds in those Christians who follow the Apostolic Mother-Churches and maintain Apostolic Succession. The heretic would merely misunderstand Scripture if quoted, so Tertullian asks the heretic to prove his orthodoxy by exhibiting a list of Apostolic Succession, showing that in a true sense the heretic followed the Apostles. The timely point of Tertullian's work *(Of Heretical Prescriptions)* is just as applicable today as it was in A.D. 200.

"This or that heresy does not receive certain Scriptures, or if it receives them, does not receive them in their integrity, but mangles them ... in order to suit its own tenets.

"Therefore with such men as these we must not appeal to Scripture, nor must we rest the issue of the controversy upon it. We must first decide the questions, to whom do the Scriptures belong? To heretics, or to the Church? To whom have they been committed? Who is their Guardian? Who is their Interpreter? Heresy, or the Church? Wheresoever the truth of Christian discipline and faith exists, there also exists, the truth of Scripture, and of the right interpretation of it, and of all Christian traditions.

"Hence it follows that every Church which agrees with those Apostolic Mother-Churches, and original sources of faith, is to be counted as true; in that it holds without wavering that true faith which the Church received from the Apostles, and which the Apostles received from Christ, and which Christ received from God.

"But let us grant, for argument's sake, that the Apostles were deceived, or even that the Holy Spirit failed to guide the Church into all truth, and to teach her all things.

"Grant all this, if you please; -what then? Is it probable, that all the Churches should have *erred into one and the same faith?* Unity is not the result of multiplicity. Error produces diversity. That which among many is found to be *one and the same*, is not an invention of error, but a tradition of truth. Did the authors of this uniform tradition err? Did error prevail uniformly in the Church, till Heresies arose to correct it? Did Truth sit patiently, like a captive in a dungeon, till some Marcionites or Valentinians arose to release her? In the meanwhile, before these heresies existed, was all preaching a mistake? Was all belief a mistake? Were the thousands of Baptisms administered up to that time a mistake? Were all ordinations, all ministrations abortive? Were all martyrdoms crowned in vain? No: Heresy is proved to be false by its novelty. The substance always precedes the shadow. Truth is always before heresy. And the Holy Scripture of Truth foretold the rise of heresies which would corrupt the truth.

"Where were the heresiarchs? Nowhere. They did not exist in the Apostles' times. Priority of time as to Christian doctrine is an evidence of truth; posteriority, a proof of falsehood. Our challenge therefore to all heresies is this — Exhibit the origin of your Churches. Unroll the succession of your Bishops. Show us that the first in order in that succession was a person (ordained) by an Apostle, or by a man who had conversed with the Apostles. Such is the pedigree and census of all Apostolic Churches; as, for example, of the Church of Smyrna were Polycarp was placed as Bishop by St. John; or of the Church of Rome, where Clement was ordained by St. Peter."

Some fifty years later (c. A.D. 250), the Bishop of Carthage, Cyprian, wrote to Cornelius, Bishop of Rome, that the unity of the Church should be preserved by bishops of Apostolic Succession. In his *Epistle to Cornelius*, Cyprian wrote, "This, Brother, is and ought to be our principal labor and study, to the utmost of our power, to take care that the unity may still obtain which was delivered by Our Lord and by His Apostles to us, their Successors."

Firmilian, Bishop of Caesarea, and friend of Cyprian, defended Cyprian in his dispute with Stephen, Bishop of Rome, over heretical Baptisms. Firmilian, in his Epistle to Cyprian, wrote of the power of remitting sins which Christ gave to the apostles. This power, according to the Bishop of Caesarea, was given to the bishops by ordination in succession from the apostles. "The power of remitting sins was given to the Apostles, and to the churches which they founded, and to the bishops who succeeded to the Apostles by a vicarious ordination."

Another Church Father, bishop in the Province of Carthage about this time, Clarus a Muscula, spoke in the Council of Carthage of the governing power of bishops. Clarus a Muscula declared that this power was held in succession from the Apostles, who in turn had received it from Our Lord:

"The sentence of Our Lord Jesus Christ is manifest, sending His Apostles, and to them alone committing the power given Him by His Father; to whom we (bishops) have succeeded, governing the Church of Our Lord with the same power."

On of the most important of the ecclesiastical historians of all time is the Bishop of Pamphilius, the learned scholar, Eusebius. In his *Ecclesiastical History* (written c. 305), Eusebius recorded much information on Apostolic Succession and gave us several lists of bishops of various sees. He spoke of these bishops as being "in the first rank of Apostolic Succession" and his lists of succession are drawn from "accounts delivered in the various comments on apostolic doctrine". Let us examine some of Eusebius' lists. We shall take four Apostolic Churches: Antioch, Alexandria, Rome and Jerusalem.

The Church of Antioch was established by St. Peter, and he was Bishop of Antioch for some time. The episcopate passed from Peter to Euodius, his successor. *Ecclesiastical History* gives us this list of Bishops of Antioch:

Bishops of Antioch

Peter the Apostle	Philetus
Euodius	Zebinus A.D. 230
Ignatius d. A.D. 110-117	Babylas A.D. 236
Heros c. A.D. 117	Fabius
Cornelius	Demetrianus
Eros	Paul
Theophilus A.D. 166	Domnus
Maximinus	Timaeus
Serapion d. A.D. 211	Cyril
Ascelepiades	Tyranus d. c. A.D. 325

The church of Alexandria was established by St. Paul, who was succeeded by St. Mark, the Gospel writer.

Bishops of Alexandria

Paul the Apostle
Mark (ante A.D. 60)
Annianus
Avilius A.D. 88
Cerdo A.D. 98
Primus A.D. 110
Justus A.D. 120
Eumenes A.D. 131
Mark II?

Celadion A.D. 152
Agrippinus A.D. 166
Julianus A.D. 180
Demetaius A.D. 193
Heraclas A.D. 236
Dionysius c. A.D. 252
Maximus c. A.D. 267
Theonas c. A.D. 285
Peter c. A.D. 304

Irenaeus, Bishop of Lyons, wrote that the Church of Rome was founded "by the *two* most glorious Apostles, Peter and Paul . . . these blessed Apostles, having founded and builded the Church, committed the ministry of the Episcopate to Linus *(Work Against Heresies)."* This Linus was a friend of (and co-prisoner with) Paul at Rome and was a native of Britain.

Bishops of Rome

Peter (and Paul) the Apostle(s)
Linus c. A.D. 61
Anencletus A.D. 79
Clement A.D. 89
Evarestus A.D. 97
Alexander A.D. 105
Xystus A.D. 115
Telesphorus A.D. 125
Hyginus A.D. 136
Pius A.D. 140
Anicetus A.D. 155
Soter A.D. 166
Eleutherus A.D. 174
Victor A.D. 189
Zephyrinus A.D. 197

Callistus A.D. 217
Urbanus A.D. 222
Pontianas A.D. 230
Anteros A.D. 236
Fabian A.D. 236
Cornelius A.D. 251
Lucius A.D. 254
Stephen A.D. 254
Xystus II A.D. 257
Dionysius A.D. 259
Felix A.D. 268
Eutychianus A.D. 273
Caius A.D. 274
Marcellinus A.D. 289

The Mother-Church of Christianity and the Chief Bishopric of the Church was Jerusalem. The Bishop of Jerusalem held a pre-eminence over all other bishops and St. James, the brother of Our Lord, was the first Bishop of Jerusalem. He presided over the first council of the Church and rendered the decision binding on all Christians. He was succeeded by one Simeon, son of Clopas.

Bishops of Jerusalem

James the Lord's brother, Apostle	Julianus A.D. 163
Simeon c. A.D. 60	Caius A.D. 165
Justus A.D. 107	Symmachus A.D. 168
Zaccheus A.D. 111	Caius II A.D. 170
Tobias A.D. 112	Julianus II A.D. 173
Benjamin A.D. 117	Maximus II A.D. 178
John A.D. 119	Antonius A.D. 182
Matthias A.D. 121	Capito A.D. 186
Philip A.D. 122	Valens A.D. 191
Seneca A.D. 126	Dolichianus A.D. 194
Justus II A.D. 127	Narcissus A.D. 195
Levi A.D. 128	Dius A.D. 200
Ephres A.D. 129	Germanio A.D. 207
Joseph A.D. 131	Gordius A.D. 211
Judas A.D. 132	Alexander A.D. 237
Mark A.D. 134	Mazabanes A.D. 251
Cassianus A.D. 146	Hymenaius A.D. 275
Publius A.D. 154	Zamboas A.D. 298
Maximus A.D. 159	Hermon A.D. 300

From these lists given in the *Ecclesiastical History* we can see that bishops have existed in the Church "from the Apostles' time" and have succeeded to their office and authority. Thus, Apostolic Succession is a historical reality as well as a theological truth.

As the Church moved into the fourth century, these traditions of ordination by bishops in Apostolic Succession were codified in canons, or church laws, passed by various Councils of the Church. The earliest canon law on ordination that has come down to us is the collection of Apostolic Canons compiled in the early fourth century from a second century work reputedly based on the canons drawn up by the Apostles themselves. The first canon of these laws or rules declared that all ministers were to be ordained by the Bishop of Apostolic Succession. "Let a Bishop be ordained by two or three Bishops: A Presbyter and a Deacon by one Bishop *(Apostolic Canons,* Canon I)." Again, we see the threefold ministry of bishop, presbyter and deacon, with the bishop as the source and authority of continuity.

In A.D. 314, a Council met at Arles, France (attended by the British Bishops of London, York and Caerleon). This Council drew up a body of canons touching upon many points of Church Order. One of these canons required three bishops to ordain another bishop and stated that no one bishop could ordain bishops without the consent of at least seven bishops. The purpose of this canon was to protect the Apostolic Succession of the Church:

> "Let no Bishop be ordained without three Bishops. If any think that he alone is sufficient for the ordination of a Bishop, let him understand that no one can presume to do this unless he has seven other Bishops associated with him *(Council of Arles, Canon XX)."*

The first Great or General Council of the Church met at Nicea, in the year 325. This Council spoke for the whole Christian Church and representatives of the whole Catholic Church were present. Again, canons were drawn up and were the law of the Universal Church. Canon IV ordered a bishop to be ordained by at least three bishops, and by all the bishops of the province, if possible:

> " A Bishop ought to be constituted by all the Bishops of the province, but if this be not practicable by reason of urgent necessity, three must by all means meet together, and with the consent of those that are absent, let them perform the ordination *(Council of Nicea,* Canon IV)."

The last Early Father we shall examine is St. Jerome, a priest, and Latin translator of the Bible. Towards the close of the fourth century (c. A.D. 385), Jerome wrote his *Epistle to Evangelum.* He speaks of all bishops being equal in power and all bishops being successors of the Apostles:

> "Wherever the Bishop be, whether at Rome, or Eugubium, or Constantinople, or Rhegium, or Alexandria, or

Tanais, his is of the same degree, and of the same Priesthood; for all are successors of the Apostles."

In this same work Jerome compared the present Christian ministry with the Jewish ministry of Old Testament times. The Christian bishop corresponds to Aaron, the high priest, the presbyters are the priests, the sons of Aaron, and the deacons are Christian levites. In this he echoes Clement of Rome three hundred years earlier.

"And we know from Apostolical tradition, taken from the Old Testament, that what Aaron, and his sons, and the Levites have been in the Temple, the same the Bishops, and the Presbyters, and the Deacons may claim as their own in the Church."

We have examined the "Ancient Authors" of the Church and have seen that they set forth substantially the same Church Order we found in Holy Scripture a threefold order of bishop, priest, and deacon. We have seen Apostolic Succession clearly set out and lists of Apostolic Succession given. In every instance the episcopate is the center of authority and power. This doctrine of Church Order existed in the first, second, third and fourth centuries. (We shall see that this order has continued to the present day.) It existed in Italy, France, Africa, Arabia, Asia Minor, and in fact in every country the Church reached.

Moreover, we have seen that Church Fathers, writing at the same time the apostles were writing the New Testament, asserted a belief in Apostolic Succession and the episcopate. Men who were personal friends and followers of the apostles wrote of the threefold ministry and the succession of bishops. Men who had known Our Lord and had been Christians from the first believed in and wrote of this Church Order of Apostolic Succession. Bishops, priests and laymen set forth a clear view of this doctrine. The great leaders and scholars of the Early Church as well as little known theologians wrote treatises on the subject. Church Councils and early Church Laws protected it. It *is* therefore evident that the threefold ministry of Apostolic Succession has indeed existed "from the Apostles' time."

Having seen that both Scripture and Fathers assert a

threefold ministry of Apostolic Succession, we must next turn to the question of whether this succession in fact has been maintained. Early lists of Apostolic Succession are easily traced and for the first years of the Church the records are fairly complete. For example, Holy Scripture tells us that Matthias succeeded Judas; and that Titus was Paul's successor at Crete even as Timothy was at Ephesus.

The Church Fathers also set out examples of Apostolic Succession. Irenaeus tells us that Linus was ordained by Peter and Paul to carry out the work of the Apostles at Rome. Tertullian stated that St. Peter also ordained Clement as third Bishop of Rome. According to Eusebius, St. Peter ordained Euodius to succeed him at Antioch. Theodoret mentions the fact that Euodius' successor, Ignatius, was also ordained by Peter. Tertullian tells us that Polycarp was ordained Bishop of Smyrna by the Apostle John and Eusebius states that Polycarp then ordained Irenaeus, who succeeded Pothinus as second Bishop of Lyons.

From these early sources we can reconstruct the probable succession of bishops. However, from the third to the sixth centuries, the records are incomplete and a true reconstruction for this period is problematic. Bearing in mind the fact that records are missing or destroyed, we may nevertheless give a fairly accurate list of succession in the Church.

For example, let us trace the succession of St. Augustine, the first Archbishop of Canterbury. This list of succession is fairly easy to reconstruct since the succession comes for the most part through the Bishops of Arles and Lyons.

Succession of St. Augustine

	St. John the Apostle
A.D. 97	Polycarp — Smyrna
Ante 166	Irenaeus — Lyons
197	Zacharias — Lyons
?	Elias — Lyons
c. 235	Trophimus — Arles
?	Faustinus — Lyons
254	Martin I — Arles
c. 266	Julius — Lyons
313	Marinus — Arles
?	Vocius — Lyons

346	Valentine — Arles
c. 353	Tetradus — Lyons
?	Artemius — Arles
374	Justus — Lyons
?	Heros — Arles
?	Sicarius — Lyons
426	Honoratus — Arles
427	Eucheius I — Lyons
449	Ravenus — Arles
451	Patiens — Lyons
?	? — Arles
?	Lupicinus — Lyons
492	Aeonius — Arles
499	Stephanus — Lyons
506	Caeserius — Arles
542	Licontius — Lyons
546	Aurelian — Arles
552	Nicetus — Lyons
557	Sepandus — Arles
573	Priscus — Lyons
588	Virgilius — Arles
596	Augustine — Canterbury

Here the succession runs out and we can trace the successors of Augustine for only about seventy five years. The last know bishop in that succession is Putta, Bishop of Rochester, who was consecrated in 669. Did he take part in any consecration? If he did no records exist and it becomes impossible to trace the succession any further. However, if we pursue the succession of French Bishops for about a century more, we find one Godwin, Bishop of Lyons, consecrating Brihtwald as eighth Archbishop of Canterbury. This Brihtwald establishes a succession that does not die out. His succession can be traced to the present day with little trouble but we must again bear in mind that the list of consecrators is a probable list for the third to sixth centuries and records are not really complete until the eleventh century or later.

Let us then trace this succession from the French Bishops of the sixth century to the American Bishops of the twentieth. We recall that Virgilius of Arles was consecrated Bishop in 588 by Priscus of Lyons. We trace the succession from that point.

Apostolic Succession

A.D.	588	Virgilius — Arles
	603	Aridius — Lyons
	613	Floriannus — Arles
	614	Hiltigisus — Toulon
	679	Felix — Arles
	680	Lambert — Lyons
	684	Volbertus — Arles
	693	Godwin — Lyons
	693	Brihtwald — Canterbury
	705	Daniel — Winchester
	731	Tatwine — Canterbury
	733	Alwig — Lindsey
	735	Nathelm — Canterbury
	736	Cuthbert — Hereford
	745	Ecgwulf — London
	766	Juenberht — Canterbury
	786	Cyneberht — Winchester
	793	Aethelheard — Canterbury
	798	Deneberht — Worcester
	805	Wulfred — Canterbury
c.	809	Wigthegn — Winchester
	833	Ceolnoth — Canterbury
	862	Alfred — Winchester
	870	Ethelred — Canterbury
	873	Wereferth — Worcester
	909	Anthelm — Wells*
	914	Wulfhelm — Wells
c.	926	Odo — Ramsbury*
	957	Dunstan — Worcester*
	985	Segeric — Ramsbury*
	990	Elfric — Ramsbury*
	1003	Wulfstan — Worcester
	1020	Ethelnoth — Canterbury
c.	1035	Eadsize — St. Martin's*
	1043	Stiganol — Elmham*
	1058	Siward — Rochester
	1070	Lanfranc — Canterbury
	1070	Thomas — York
	1093	Anselm — Canterbury
	1107	Roger — Salisbury

1139 Theobald — Canterbury
1148 Foliot — Hereford
1176 de Leis — St. David's
1189 Fitz Walter — Salisbury*
1199 William — London
1214 de Gray — Worcester
1249 Kirkham — Durham
1255 Henry — Whithern
1292 Halton — Carlisle
1322 Northburgh — Lichfield
1330 Wyvill — Salisbury
1362 Sudbury — London*
1374 Arundel — Ely*
1408 Nicholls — Bangor
1425 Stafford — Bath*
1435 Bourchier — Worcester*
1479 Morton — Ely*
1487 Fox — Exeter
1502 Warham — London*
1521 Longlands — Lincoln
1530 Stokesley — London
1537 Hodgkin — Suffr. of Bedford
1559 Grindal — London*
1577 Whitgift — Worcester*
1597 Bancroft — London*
1609 Abbot — Lichfield*
1616 Morton — Chester
1619 Howson — Oxford
1621 Laud — St. David's*
1635 Wren — Hereford
1660 Morley — Worcester
1661 Sharpe — St. Andrew's
1663 Burnet — Glasgow
1675 Patterson — Glasgow
1705 Fullarton — Edinburgh
1722 Cant (No Diocese)
1727 Rattray — Dunkeld
1741 Falconer — Moray
1768 Kilgour — Aberdeen
1784 Seabury — Connecticut+
1792 Claggett — Maryland
1797 Bass — Massachusetts

1797 Jarvis — Connecticut
1811 Griswold — Eastern Diocese+
1832 Hopkins — Vermont+
1867 Tuttle — Montana+
1911 Perry — Rhode Island+
1930 Sherrill — Massachusetts+
1951 Lichtenberger Missouri+
1961 Allin — Mississippi+

>*denotes elevation to Archbishop of Canterbury.
>+denotes elevation to Presiding Bishop of the United States.

Thus we can see a continuous succession of bishops from the Apostles to the present day: an *Apostolic* succession.

Historically, the Church has always believed in Apostolic Succession and the episcopate as one of the essential marks of the Church. Nonetheless, it is also important to trace the teaching of Anglican Church Fathers in this area, especially in view of the confusion of the Reformation period. The great Reformers of the Anglican Church, Cranmer, Latimer, Shaxton, Stokesby, Tonstall, Sampson and others, issued a joint statement on Ordination, Succession, and Orders in 1536, just two years after the beginning of the final stage of the Reformation:

> "Christ and His Apostles did institute and ordain in the New Testament certain ministers or officers, which should bear spiritual power, authority, and commission under Christ, to preach and teach the word of God unto His people; to dispense and administer the Sacraments of God unto them, and by the same to confer and give the grace of the Holy Ghost; to consecrate the blessed Body of Christ in the Sacrament of the Altar; to loose and absolve from sin all persons which be duly penitent and sorry for the same; to bind and ex-communicate such as be guilty in manifest crimes and sins, and will not amend their defaults; to order and consecrate others in the same room, order, and office, whereunto they be called and admitted themselves . . .

> "This office, this power and authority, was committed and given by Christ and His Apostles unto certain per-

sons only, that is to say, unto Priests or Bishops, whom they did elect, call and admit thereunto by their prayer and imposition of their hands . . .

"The invisible gift of grace conferred in this Sacrament is nothing else but the power, office, and authority before mentioned; the visible and outward sign is the prayer and imposition of the Bishop's hands, upon the person which receiveth the said gift of grace.

"And to the intent the Church of Christ should never be destituted of such Ministers, as should have and execute the said power of the keys; it was also ordained and commanded by the Apostles, that the same Sacrament (of Holy Orders) should be applied and minstered by the Bishop from time to time, and unto such other persons as had the qualities, which the Apostles very diligently describe, as it appeareth in the first Epistle of St. Paul to Timothy, and his Epistle to Titus."

Twelve years later, on the eve of the publication of the first Prayer book, Archbishop Cranmer reiterated the idea of Apostolic Succession in his sermon, "Power of the Keys." Cranmer, the leader of the English reforms, and reputedly the principal author of *The Book of Common Prayer*, firmly believed in Apostolic Succession, as the sermon delivered in 1548, indicates:

"The ministrations of God's word, which our Lord Jesus Christ Himself at first did institute, was derived from the Apostles unto others after them, by imposition of hands, and giving the Holy Ghost, from the Apostles' time to our days, and this was the consecration, orders, and unction of the Apostles, whereby they, at the beginning, made Bishops and Priests, and this shall continue in the Church even to the world's end."

Two years later, in 1550, the first official statement of the Church of England was set forth on the Ministry: *the Preface to the Ordinal*. The *Preface to the Ordinal* of 1550 stated clearly the belief of the Church in the Catholic threefold ministry, the intention of continuing that ministry, and the belief in Episcopal Succession as the only means of continuity allowed:

"It is evident to all men diligently reading Holy Scripture and ancient Authors, that from the Apostles' time there have been these Orders of Ministers in Christ's Church: Bishops, Priests and Deacons.

"... And, therefore, to the intent that these Orders may be continued and reverently used in the Church of England; no man shall be accounted or taken to be a lawful Bishop, Priest, or Deacon in the Church of England, or suffered to execute any of the said functions ... except he hath had Episcopal Consecration or Ordination."

Eight years later, at the close of the reign of Mary Tudor, the reforming bishops of the Church again affirmed their belief in Apostolic Succession. In a Council held in 1558, seven Anglican Fathers (Scory, Grindal, Cox, Elmer, Guest, Jewell and Horn) stated: "The Apostles' authority is derived upon after ages, and conveyed to the Bishops their Successors."

In 1593, Thomas Bilson, later Bishop of Winchester, wrote in his *Perpetual Government of Christ's Church* that the Sacramental power of the Church could be exercised only by ministers of Apostolic Succession:

"To preach, baptize, retain sins, and impose hands, princes have no power; the Prince of princes, even the Son of God, hath severed it from their calling, and committed it to His Apostles; and they by imposition of hands derived it to their successors."

One of the greatest thinkers of the Anglican Church, the saintly Richard Hooker, declared in his *Ecclesiastical Polity* that the bishop, according to the Ancient Church, is of the *esse* of the Church:

"It was the general received persuasion of the ancient Christian world that 'Ecclesia est in episcopo,' the outward being of a Church consisted in the having of a bishop."

Hooker went on to state a belief in the continued existence of Apostolic Succession in the Church when he said that ministers are in "a lineal descent of power from the Apostles by continued succession of bishops in every effectual ordination."

The last of the sixteenth century Reformers we shall examine is John Overall, Bishop of Lichfield, who set forth the eternal continuity of episcopal ordinations in Apostolic Succession in his *Convocation Book:*

> "(Part of) the episcopal function (is) to ordain, by the authority of the Apostles give unto them, other ministers to succeed themselves; that so the said Apostolic Authority, being derived in that sort from one to another, there might never be any want of pastors and teachers . . . unto the end of the world."

At the beginning of the seventeenth century, Francis Mason, in his *Vindication of the Church of England,* stated that the power of the priesthood was given by Apostolic Succession: "The Priesthood which the Apostles conferred was . . . a spiritual power to minister the Word and Sacraments . . . conveyed to posterity successively by ordination." Mason went on to point out that this Succession began in Christ, through the apostles, and was passed on down through the ages by the bishops. "Christ himself is the author of our orders, from whom the power of ordaining others, flowing as from a pure fountain first to the Apostles, next, from the Apostles, ran down to the bishops as its conduit-pipes."

John Pearson, the learned Bishop of Chester, wrote that the power of the ministry was of Divine origin. He stated that the Father sent Christ, Christ sent the apostles, and the apostles sent their successors, the bishops. Further no one can send or ordain, unless he first has been ordained and sent, nor can he give anything but what he has received:

> "And this is what makes effective the works of the ministry, that all is attributed to Divine virtue . . . The Bishop confers Holy Orders . . . As the Father sent Christ, so Christ sent the apostles, and the apostles their successors . . . And the fact is, no one can send except he be sent, no one can ordain except he be ordained, no one can give except he has first received *(Minor Works* Translation by author)."

The Great Jeremy Taylor, Irish Bishop of Down and Connor, also ably defended the doctrine of Apostolic Succession.

Taylor lived through the attempt of Protestants to destroy the episcopate of the Church in the British Isles and was especially aware of the importance of Apostolic Succession. In his *Works* he argues that the Apostolate is perpetual through succession:

> "That the apostolate might be successive and perpetual, Christ gave them a power of ordination, that by imposing hands on others, they might impart that power which they received from Christ."

Taylor goes on to say that the apostles had this power of the priesthood, and its protection was found in the episcopate:

> "These (the power to govern the Church, to administer Sacraments, to preach, and to ordain) the Apostles had without all question; and whatsoever they had, they had from Christ, and these were eternally necessary; these, then, were the offices of the Apostolate, which Christ promised to assist forever, and that is what we now call the order and office of episcopacy."

Here, then, we have the assertion that the episcopate is of the *esse* of the Church — "these (the episcopal powers) were eternally necessary."

Another seventeenth century Anglican Divine was John Scott, who said that the government of the Church was the episcopate in Apostolic Succession:

> "(There is) a standing form of government and discipline in the Church, instituted by our Savior himself, which ... is this, that there should be an episcopacy, or order of men, authorized in a continued succession from the Apostles (who were authorized by Himself)" *(Works)*.

Scott went on to emphasize the definite apostolic nature of episcopacy, describing it as, "Nothing else but only the Apostolical superiority derived from the hands of the Apostles in a continued succession from one generation to another."

The Bishop of Worcester, Edward Stillingfleet, believed Apostolic Succession was a "divine institution." He said, "There is as great reason to believe the Apostolical Succession to be of divine institution, as the canon of Scripture, or the observation of the Lord's Day." *(Works).*

In the eighteenth century, George Horne wrote that the Sacraments depended upon Apostolic Succession:

> "(The Sacraments) can no man minister to effect but by God's own appointment; at first by his immediate appointment, and afterwards by succession and derivation from thence to the end of the world." *(Works).*

William Jones of Nayland, writing in the same century, stated plainly that the threefold Catholic Ministry of Apostolic Succession was one of the marks of the Church, that this was of the esse:

> "The Church has been governed by bishops, priests, and deacons from the Apostles downwards; and where we find these orders of ministers duly appointed, the word preached, and the sacraments administered, there we find the Church of Christ, with its form and its authority" *(Works).*

One of the most important Bishops of the Early American Church was William White, first Bishop of Pennsylvania. Consecrated to the episcopal office in the eighteenth century, he continued to lead the Church in the opening years of the nineteenth. In his *Opinions on Interchanging With Ministers of Non-Episcopal Communion,* White states:

> "The divine institution of the ministry is as conspicuous a fact as any in sacred history. When our Savior gave His commission, . . . it was not to His disciples at large, but to those whom He had before appointed His Apostles . . . All subsequent introduction to the ministry . . . was by the hands of and in succession from the Apostles, thus divinely designated."

In 1886, the House of Bishops of the Episcopal Church made a declaration of minimum points of the Faith *necessary* for Christian Unity. This declaration, called the Chicago Quadrilateral, affirmed that "the Christian Unity now so earnestly desired . . . can be restored only by the return . . . to the principles of unity exemplified by the undivided Catholic

Church during the first ages of its existence; which principles we believe to be the substantial deposit of Christian Faith and Order committed by Christ and his Apostles to the Church unto the end of the world, and therefore incapable of compromise or surrender... "As (an) inherent (part) of this sacred deposit, and therefore as essential to the restoration of unity ... we account ... the Historic Episcopate ..."

The Lambeth Conference of 1888 adopted the Quadrilateral for the whole Anglican Communion and the 1930 Lambeth Conference re-affirmed the so-called Chicago-Lambeth Quadrilateral, by stating that: "The Historic Episcopate, as we understand it, goes behind the perversions of history to the original conception of the Apostolic Ministry."

In 1947, *Catholicity*, a report to the Archbishop of Canterbury on the conflict of Christian traditions in the West, interpreted the 1930 Report of Lambeth by stating:

> "The appeal to the *historic Episcopate* will mean the recovery of the true place of the Bishop in the Church, not as the organiser of a vast administrative machine, but as the guardian and exponent of the faith, as the bond of sacramental unity, and as an organ of the Body of Christ in true constitutional relation to the presbyters and people."

In 1982, the General Convention of the Episcopal Church declared, "We understand the historic episcopate as ... *essential* to the reunion of the Church ... Bishops in apostolic succession are, therefore, the focus and personal symbols of (apostolicity)." (Emphasis added.)

These statements of belief made by the Anglican Churches in the nineteenth and twentieth centuries, simply echo the earlier statements of Anglican theologians.

Turning from the continuous series of statements by leading bishops and theologians of the Church in every century since the Reformation, we next look at the official laws, canons and rubrics of the Church to see the officially proclaimed doctrine of the Church.

The *Preface to the Ordinal*, an official statement of the Anglican Church on the ministry, states in no uncertain terms the idea of a threefold ministry, continued in succession through the episcopate. The *Preface* further declares that only ministers of Apostolic Succession are to serve in the Church, that non-episcopally trained ministers, though godly men, are not to be counted as Ministers of God's Church in the Apostolic tradition.

The *Preface* of 1550 stated that:

> "No man shall be accounted or taken to be a lawful Bishop, Priest, or Deacon, in the Church of England, or suffered to execute any of the said Functions, except he ... hath had Episcopal Consecration or Ordination."

A hundred years later, in 1662, the Parliament of England prohibited non-episcopally ordained men from serving as ministers in the Church:

> "No person (is) to have any cure of souls, or any ecclesiastical dignity, in the Church of England, but such who had been or should be ordained priest or deacon by some bishop ... " *(Act of Uniformity,* 14 Car. II c. 4).

In America, the canon law of the Episcopal Church declared that non-episcopally ordained ministers must be reordained. Title III, Canon 12, Section 5 (a) (2) of the *Constitution and Canons*, states that in regard to a minister ordained in Churches not in communion with the Episcopal Church, the bishop may "Confirm him and make him a Deacon and ... ordain him as Priest if he has not received such ordination."

While the Anglican Churches do not recognize non-episcopally ordained ministers as having Catholic Orders, the Church does recognize the validity of Orders of all other Churches which have maintained the Apostolic Succession in the episcopate. This is what the *Preface* refers to as "Episcopal Consecration."

In 1571, Parliamentary Law in England provided for the recognition of ministers episcopally ordained by other Churches (specifically, the Church of Rome):

> "That the Churches of the Queen's Majesty's dominions may be served with pastors of sound religion, be it enacted ... that every person under the degree of a bishop which does or shall pretend (i.e. claim) to be a priest or minister of God's holy word and sacraments by any other form of institution, consecration, or ordering

than the form set forth by Parliament (i.e. by the Roman Ordinal)... before the feast of the nativity of Christ next following shall in the presence of the bishop or guardian of the spiritualities of some one diocese where he has or shall have ecclesiastical living declare his assent and subscribe to all the articles of religion which only concern the confession of the True Christian faith and the doctrine of the sacraments comprised in a book entitled: Articles, et." *(Ordination of Ministers Act,* 13 Eliz. c. 12).

Likewise, the Episcopal Church provides for a recognition of episcopal orders of non-Anglicans:

"(T)he Bishop ... may (r)eceive him ... as a Priest, if he has already been ordained by a Bishop in the historic succession." *(Constitution and Canons,* Title III, Canon 12, Section 5 (a) (1)).

The American Church canon law further provides that if a man is episcopally ordained, but the validity of the ordaining bishop is doubtful, the minister is to be conditionally ordained:

"(T)he Bishop ... may ordain him a Priest conditionally ... if he has been ordained by a Bishop whose authority to convey such orders has not been recognized by this Church." *(Constitutions and Canons,* Title III, Canon 12, Section 5 (a) (3)).

The Law of the Church, then, states clearly that only ministers of the historic succession from the Apostles are authorized to function in the Church. Episcopal ordination is recognized as the means of a valid ministry even in other Churches; specifically in the Church of Rome, the Orthodox Churches, certain Scandinavian Lutheran Churches and the Old Catholic Churches. It is therefore obvious that the Anglican Communion has always believed in Apostolic Succession and the episcopate and that the Catholic doctrine of the ministry is taught, not only by individuals, but has always been taught by the law of the Church itself.

Afterwords

As the "Detroit Report" says in the section entitled *Principles of Unity:*

"The Gospel calls us to unity in God's Church. But even a partial view of the Church, conditioned by time and history, reveals to us a broken fellowship among those who confess one Lord, one Faith, one Baptism. Created and called by God to be an instrument of the saving and liberating mission of Jesus Christ in the world, this fellowship is nonetheless visibly divided, its purpose obscured, its mission impeded, and its witness weakened.

The Episcopal Church longs for and actively seeks the unity for which our Savior prayed. For almost a century that search has been guided by the bold vision of our forefathers, set forth in what we know as the Chicago-Lambeth Quadrilateral of 1886, 1888. It has been the major criterion by which our ecumenical conversations have been established and pursued."

In the four sections of this book we have carefully reviewed the teaching of the Church as set forth in the words of Holy Scripture, the early Fathers, Catholic Tradition, and the latest formularies of the Anglican Communion. We have seen what constitutes the essence of the Faith. Christian unity, then, may be found in a "return . . . to the principles of unity exemplified by the undivided Catholic Church . . . " Those principles are contained in the four Foundations of the Faith: Scripture, Creeds, Sacraments and Ministry, the Chicago-Lambeth Quadrilateral, the "major criterion by which our ecumenical conversations have been established and pursued." As we more clearly realize how completely we have been blessed with the essentials of the Christian Religion, we will more faithfully preserve them, teach them, and spread them among all Christians. If we really believe that Christian unity "can be restored only by the return of all Christian communions to the principles of unity exemplified by the undivided Catholic Church" and if we also believe those principles "to be the substantial deposit of Christian Faith and Order committed by Christ and his Apostles to the Church unto the end of the world," then we must surely protect, preserve, understand, teach and spread that substantial deposit of Faith, for it is solemnly declared to be "incapable of compromise or surrender by those who have been ordained to be its stewards and trustees for the common and equal benefit of all men."

Only by grasping these essential Foundations of the Faith (Scripture, Creeds, Sacraments and Ministry) can we seek true lasting union. We are called to that union by Our Lord, himself, as the "Detroit Report" declares:

> "Our Lord continues to call us to make visible the unity He has given the Church. His Prayer is 'that they may all be one; even as thou, Father, art in me, and I in thee, that they may also be in us, so that the world may believe.' We hear this call in Holy Scripture and the tradition of the Church, through the needs of human kind, and through the good things happening in the ecumenical movement. The call comes with increased urgency because of forces of disunity and destruction at work today in the churches and in society."

Thus, strengthened by Faith and united in Love, we may pray our Hope:

> "Almighty Father, whose blessed Son before his passion prayed for his disciples that they might be one, as you and he are one: Grant that your Church, being bound together in love and obedience to you, may be united in one body by the one Spirit, that the world may believe in him whom you have sent, your Son Jesus Christ our Lord; who lives and reigns with you, in the unity of the Holy Spirit, one God, now and for ever. Amen.

Appendix: "Dialogues" and
Foundations of the Faith

I

In a report released in the middle of March, our church's Standing Commission on Ecumenical Relations affirmed that Lutheran piety and sacramental practice do meet the requirements of eucharistic sharing as approved by General Convention in 1967 and 1979 [TLC, Apr. 19].

The commission voted to recommend that the 1982 convention extend eucharistic hospitality to members of the four Lutheran churches participating in the dialogue with the Episcopal Church. The commission also expressed the hope that the Lutherans would extend similar hospitality to Episcopalians and that entire congregations of both churches might be involved in worship and celebrations of the Eucharist with each other.

Contrary to the impression given that this is some new, important concept of ecumenical breakthrough, the proposal is at least nine years old. The same suggestions for interim eucharistic sharing were put forward in the *Lutheran-Episcopal Dialogue, A Progress Report,* published by the Forward Movement in 1972. (For example, see statements 85, 86 and 87, page 161 of the report.)

Specifically, statement 85 proclaims that the Anglican

This article originally appeared in *The Living Church* on May 24, 1982. Used by permission.

members "wish to declare that they see in the Lutheran Communion true proclamation of the Word and celebration of the sacraments." Statement 86 sees this as implying "official encouragement of intercommunion in forms appropriate to local conditions." Finally, statement 87 says, "The Anglican participants cannot foresee full integration of ministries (full communion) apart from the historic episcopate, but this should in no sense preclude increasing inter-communion between us . . . "

Can Episcopalians properly receive communion at an altar where the celebrant is not a priest ordained by a bishop in Apostolic Succession? Can we officially sanction such a practice? These are the questions raised by the "Interim Eucharistic Fellowship."

The same questions were raised in the Detroit Report of the National Ecumenical Consultation of the Episcopal Church in November of 1978. The report stated that the "Dialogue reports and the survey of these discussions written for this Consultation have not made fully explicit the reasons why our participants in the Lutheran-Episcopal Dialogue find it possible for us to engage in eucharistic sharing with Lutheran Churches in the Lutheran-Episcopal Dialogue prior to their acceptance of the historic episcopate, nor how this could be done without thereby implying that the historic episcopate is for us *adiaphora*, nor why such an action would not in principle be applicable to all Protestant churches of a creedal/confessional nature" [TLC, Jan. 21, 1979].

Indeed, how can we consider such a proposal without declaring, at least implicitly, that priesthood in the apostolic succession is no longer one of the essential elements of the Eucharist?

The *Preface to the Ordination Rites* of the Prayer Book (page 510), speaking of priests, declares that, "Together with the bishops, they take part in administering [God's] holy Sacraments." The 1928 Prayer Book, on page 294, says essentially the same thing, in proclaiming that the "office of a Priest is . . . to celebrate the Holy Communion." The 1979 book goes on to declare (page 510) that "No persons are allowed to exercise the offices of bishop, priest, or deacon in this Church unless they . . . have . . . received . . . ordination with the laying on of hands by bishops who are themselves duly qualified to confer Holy Orders."

Our national canon law makes clear provisions for ministers ordained in churches not in communion with this church, in Canon III.12. 5 *(Constitution and Canons,* 1979, page 76). Before such a minister may function in this church as a priest *(i.e.,* celebrate the Eucharist) he must (1) be received by a bishop of this church as a priest, "if he has already been ordained by a Bishop in the historic succession;" or (2) be ordained a deacon and then a priest, "if he has not received such ordination"; or (3) be ordained conditionally, "if he has been ordained by a Bishop whose authority to convey such orders has not been recognized by this Church."

Clearly, then, the official teaching and law of the Episcopal Church insist upon ordination by a bishop in Apostolic Succession as a prerequisite to functioning as the celebrant at the altar. This only affirms what the Episcopal Church has always said. The Chicago Quadrilateral, adopted by the House of Bishops in 1886, ratified by the Lambeth Conference of 1888, and now printed in the Prayer Book (pages 876, 877), declares:

> We do herby affirm that the Christian unity ... can be restored only by the return of all Christian communions to the principles of unity exemplified by the undivided Catholic Church during the first ages of its existence; which principles we believe to be ... incapable of compromise or surrender ...
>
> As inherent parts of this sacred deposit, and therefore as essential to the restoration of unity among the divided branches of Christendom, we account the ... Historic Episcopate ...

As the Detroit Report said of the Historic Episcopate of Apostolic Succession:

> Apostolic *ministry* exists to promote, safeguard, and serve apostolic teaching. All Christians are called into this ministry by their Baptism. In order to serve, lead, and enable this ministry, some are set apart and ordained in the historic orders of Bishop, Presbyter, and Deacon. We understand the historic episcopate as central to this apostolic ministry and to the reunion of Christendom ... Bishops in apostolic succession are, therefore, the focus and personal symbols of this inheritance ...

In dealing with both Protestants and Roman Catholics, the Episcopal Church has consistently held that the Eucharist must be celebrated by a priest (or bishop), and no other. for example, we read in the A/RC Agreed Statement on Ministry and Ordination (Section 9):

> Presbyters are joined with the Bishop . . . in the ministry of the word and the sacraments; they are given authority to preside at the Eucharist . . . Deacons (are) not so empowered . . . (Adopted by 1979 General Convention, Resolution A-37).

The same stand was taken in regard to the Eucharist and Protestant Churches in the COCU Resolution (A-41) which authorized the participation of Episcopalians in the COCU Eucharist "provided that an ordained priest of this Church is the celebrant, or one of the celebrants at a con-celebrated service." On some occasions, this arrangement may indeed offer a more constructive approach.

Among Lutherans, the historic episcopate has been preserved in a few cases: Most Lutheran Churches have either never had this succession, or have not continued it (Statement 80, *Lutheran-Episcopal Dialogue*, page 160).

While there may be some Lutheran pastors in America who have been ordained by Lutheran bishops in Europe in the historic succession, no Lutheran Churches in the United States possess the historic episcopate. To enter into a limited or interim eucharistic sharing with these churches is to encourage our people to receive at altars presided over by persons who are not priests.

It has been argued by our participants in the dialogue that there is precedent for being communicated by a non-episcopally ordained minister *(Dialogue Report,* page 40) inasmuch as the Lutherans were not *able* to preserve the historic episcopate outside of Scandinavia, through no fault of their own *(ibid,* pages 21, 40, 41).

This was admittedly true, *but only at the time of the Reformation.* We are reminded that the Philippine Independent Church was unable to preserve the historic episcopate at the time of its schism with Rome. However, in 1948, the Episcopal Church consecrated bishops for that church, and today all its ministers are in the historic succession. The same is true of the Lusitanian Church and the Spanish Reformed Churches, now integral parts of the Anglican Communion.

Since the Lutheran Churches are now capable of obtaining the historic episcopate from their own Lutheran bishops in Sweden, and since the Anglican Communion has already declared to both Roman Catholics and Protestants that the priest in Apostolic Succession is the proper minister of the Eucharist, there is no logical reason to support the notion of any "interim eucharistic sharing" apart from the historic episcopate of Apostolic Succession.

The problem is that Lutherans are not yet willing to accept the Anglican position on the historic succession. Lutherans claim that the important part of Apostolic Succession is the succession of doctrine, and that the succession of persons is meaningless. Again quoting from the *Lutheran-Episcopal Dialogue*, page 107:

> Doctrine never dies, and wherever it goes there is the true Church, the true bishops, the true priests. Where it is not present any other kind of succesion is an empty grave of the prophets, an empty vessel, a vessel filled with mould and rottenness (Matthew 23:25-28). If we have only this succession of doctrine we shall not lack the power and vitality to prove even before the eyes of men, that a church is there. This is the succession for which we must strive, and then we shall lack *nothing*, least of all the orderly calling of ministers, the laying on of hands, prayer, and the blessing and gifts of the Holy Spirit for those in holy office.

The Lutheran emphasis on sound doctrine is admirable. We Episcopalians can learn and benefit from it. At the same time, however, we respectfully believe that our Lutheran friends can also learn and benefit from our heritage, with its emphasis on continuity of order and sacramentality.

Perhaps the real solution to the problem is found in the Detroit Report, in its definition of apostolicity:

> A mutual recognition that apostolicity is evidenced in continuity with the teaching, the ministry, and the mission of the apostles. Apostolic *teaching* must be founded upon the Holy Scriptures and the ancient fathers and creeds, drawing its proclamation of Jesus Christ and

His Gospel for each new age from these sources, not merely reproducing them in a transmission of verbal identity.

Apostolic *ministry* exists to promote, safeguard, and serve apostolic teaching. All Christians are called into this ministry by their Baptism. In order to serve, lead, and enable this ministry, some are set apart and ordained in the historic orders of Bishop, Presbyter, and Deacon. We understand the historic episcopate as central to this apostolic ministry and to the reunion of Christendom.

Apostolic *mission* is itself a succession of apostolic teaching and ministry inherited from the past and carried into the present and future. Bishops in apostolic succession are, therefore, the focus and personal symbols of this inheritance and mission as they preach and teach the Gospel and summon the people of God to their mission of worhip and service.

It therefore would appear that the solution to the question is not *either* succession of ministry *or* succession of teaching, but *both* succession of ministry *and* succession of teaching.

Certainly, in this instance, Anglican comprehensiveness makes more sense than Lutheran exclusiveness. Lutherans insist that eucharistic sharing must come *before* agreement on the succession *(Dialogue,* page 41). Such insistence is unacceptable, and we should be honest enough to say so to our Lutheran friends.

To accept the "interim eucharistic sharing" proposal is to violate the law of the Episcopal Church, violate the spirit of our agreements with Roman Catholics and other churches we have dealt with, deny the Lambeth Quadrilateral, and reject the clear and proper definition of apostolicity put forth by the Detroit Report.

Let us be as honest with ourselves and our Lutheran brethren as we have been with others, and recognize that eucharistic sharing, interim or otherwise, is dependent upon a mutually accepted ministry. That ministry must be the historic episcopate. Until that is accepted by the Lutherans, we cannot consider eucharistic sharing.

II

Following the numerous comments flowing from my previous article "Interim Eucharistic Fellowship" [TLC, May 24], and the response of the Rev. David A. Gustafson, "A Lutheran Responds to Bishop Wantland" [TLC, Oct. 4], there has been a strong request from a number of people to continue the Anglican-Lutheran dialogue.

That continuation should focus on the question of the apostolicity of the church. Both Lutherans and Anglicans agree that apostolicity is essential to any eucharistic sharing. That apostolicity involves at least three things: apostolic teaching, apostolic ministry and apostolic mission *(Detroit Report,* November, 1978).

Contrary to the opinion expressed by Pastor Gustafson, both the Episcopal Church and I feel that these are *all* essential to Apostolic Succession. Unfortunately, the good Lutheran pastor assumes that I am maintaining "a very open-ended view on matters of doctrine and theology." To the contrary, as I said in my previous article, "It therefore would appear that the solution to the question is not *either* succession of ministry *or* succession of teaching, but *both* succession of ministry *and* succession of teaching."

Pastor Gustafson still wants to make it *either . . . or*, when he says that "the concept of apostolic succession is a broad one, and . . . both churches have, in their own way, maintained the succession."

Neither the Lutherans nor the Anglicans can afford to take that position. We are already bound to insist upon the tactual succession of the historic episcopate. This the Lutherans must accept if we are to be truly honest with each other. The Lutherans are also bound to insist upon purity of doctrine if they are to be honest with us. We Anglicans must accept this point.

Let us, therefore, take the question raised by Pastor Gustaf-

This article originally appeared in *The Living Church* on January 24, 1982. Used by permission.

son: "What would happen to the dialogues if Lutherans were to take a similar attitude with regard to doctrinal purity and insist without compromising, that Episcopalians be more consistent in their doctrine?"

I submit that the Episcopal Church would greatly benefit. For too long Anglicans have been seen as fuzzy in their thinking, allowing just about any view imaginable. It is high time for us to state precisely where the church really stands, and what is its minimum essential deposit of faith, about which there can be no compromise. It might even be high time to tell some of our bishops, priests, deacons and laity that if they persist in teaching false doctrine, they will have to leave the church.

This then raises the question of whether there *is* any clear teaching of the Episcopal Church. In spite of the irresponsible claims of a number of "loose" theologians, the answer is a loud "yes." There is a sharp, clean statement of belief binding upon all Anglicans and easily determined.

Article X of the Constitution of the Episcopal Church declares: "The . . . Articles of Religion, as now established or hereafter amended by the authority of this church, shall be in use in all the dioceses and missionary dioceses . . . of this church."

Contrary to the opinion often erroneously expressed, the Articles of Religion are binding upon the American church, just as they are binding upon the rest of the Anglican Communion. Indeed, beginning at page 867 of the Prayer Book, we find the Articles of Religion "as established by the bishops, the clergy, and the laity of the Protestant Episcopal Church in the United States of America, in convention, on the twelfth day of September, in the year of our Lord, 1801."

Those Articles of Religion spell out many of the essential beliefs of the church, and direct us to other authorities of the faith. For example, Article VI declares: "Holy Scripture containeth all things necessary to salvation so that whatsoever is not read therein, nor may be proved thereby, is not to be required of any man, that it should be believed as an article of the faith, or be thought requisite or necessary to salvation . . ."

Article VIII states: "The Nicene Creed, and that which is commonly called the Apostles' Creed, ought thoroughly to be received and believed; for they may be proved by most certain warrants of Holy Scripture."

There you have the foundation of our doctrine — Holy Scripture and the historic creeds. These are binding upon Anglicans, and those who teach contrary to Scripture or the articles of faith in the creeds are in error, and depart from the teachings of the church.

As to the nature of God, Article I insists upon full belief in the Holy Trinity. Article II insists upon the fully human and divine nature of Christ, upon the Incarnation and virgin birth, and the reality of his suffering and death for us. His Resurrection and Ascension are clearly taught and required of belief in Article IV.

We could go on, and quote from the Catechism ("An Outline of the Faith") beginning on page 845 of the Prayer Book. This, also, is a clear statement of the essentials of the Christian faith. In fact, one of the uses of the Catechism "is to provide a brief summary of the church's teaching" (p. 844). This Catechism, an integral part of the Prayer Book, is also binding upon the church by virtue of the provisions of Article X of the church's Constitution.

To the Scriptures and creeds (and Articles of Religion and of Catechism) can be added other documents of teaching which are binding upon the Anglican Communion. These include the ecumenical councils of the undivided church. (The first six councils are recognized as binding upon Anglicans by virtue of the homily entitled "Against Peril of Idolatry," approved by Article XXXV. For the seventh council, see note one, page 137, volume II of *Dogmatic Theology*, by Francis J. Hall, entitled "Authority.")

If there is a clear statement of the articles of faith required of belief by Anglicans, what about those ministers of the Episcopal Church who are (as Gustafson says) Calvinist or Zwinglian heretics? Can their ordinations redeem their defective theology, or are their sacramental ministrations utterly invalid?

Again, we are directed to the Articles of Religion, Article XXVI: "Although in the visible church the evil be ever mingled with the good, and sometimes the evil have chief authority in the ministration of the Word and sacraments, yet forasmuch as they do not the same in their own name, but in Christ's, and do minister by his commission and authority, we may use their ministry, both in hearing the Word of God, and in receiving the sacraments.

"Neither is the effect of Christ's ordinance taken away by their wickedness, nor the grace of God's gifts diminished from such as by faith, and rightly, do receive the sacraments ministered unto them; which be effectual, because of Christ's institution and promise, although they be ministered by evil men."

Thus, the sacramental acts of heretical priests (or bishops) are not necessarily invalidated by their heresy. However, we Anglicans have for too long overlooked the rest of Article XXVI. We have a responsibility to discharge in regard to the false teachers in the church: "Nevertheless, it appertaineth to the discipline of the church, that inquiry be made of evil ministers, and that they be accused by those that have knowledge of their offenses, and finally, being found guilty, by just judgment be deposed."

Let us, as Anglicans, start putting our house in order and quit tolerating false doctrine. Let us restore discipline. Certainly, as an Anglican, I must admit that Pastor Gustafson is correct when he says, "To Lutherans, it appears that the Episcopal Church allows much more doctrinal latitude than would be tolerated within their own church body. One finds a range of theological positions that boggles the mind of one who is a part of a more doctrinally confessional body."

We Anglicans must begin to reassert the truths we hold essential, and to repudiate those heretical and speculative views which fly in the face of these essential truths. The Episcopal Church *officially* teaches all the necessary articles of the catholic faith, and does not *officially* teach anything as required of belief that is heretical.

However, we have misled our friends of other Christian bodies by our looseness of discipline, and our unwillingness to say to our own people, "What you say is simply wrong, and if you are going to speak for the church, you must cease and desist in proclaiming as truth what the church declares is false." I am not proposing a return to the Inquisition, but I am proposing a return to intellectual honesty and dogmatic integrity.

I am saying precisely what Pastor Gustafson shrank from saying: We must insist upon the tactual succession as a part of the essential nature of apostolicity, and the Lutherans must likewise insist upon succession of right doctrine as a part of the essential nature of apostolicity. If either of these is lacking, there is no valid Apostolic Succession.

In order for the dialogue to continue and to bear true fruit, we Anglicans must say to our Lutheran brethren, "You must institute the historic episcopate before we can have eucharistic sharing." And the Lutherans must say to us, "You must put your doctrinal house in order, and openly proclaim the right teaching of the catholic faith before we can have eucharistic sharing."

To this end, I agree with Pastor Gustafson when he says, "I think the best way to approach the dialogues, eucharistic hospitality, and possible intercommunion is to see ourselves as mutually sinful, with shortcomings." I further agree "that Episcopalians can profit from Lutheranism's strong doctrinal stance. Lutherans should be more open to the Episcopal concern for orders."

I am therefore drawn back to that excellent statement on apostolicity in the *Detroit Report:* "Apostolic *teaching* must be founded upon the Holy Scriptures and the ancient fathers and creeds, drawing its proclamation of Jesus Christ and his Gospel for each new age from these sources, not merely reproducing them in a transmission of verbal identity.

"Apostolic *ministry* exists to promote, safeguard, and serve apostolic teaching. All Christians are called into this ministry by their Baptism. In order to serve, lead, and enable this ministry, some are set apart and ordained in the historic orders of bishop, presbyter, and deacon. We understand the historic episcopate as central to this apostolic ministry and to the reunion of Christendom.

"Apostolic *mission* is itself a succession of apostolic teaching and ministry inherited from the past and carried into the present and future. Bishops in apostolic succession are, therefore, the focus and personal symbols of this inheritance and mission as they preach and teach the Gospel and summon the people of God to their mission of worhip and service."

It is therefore clear that the solution to the question is not *either* succession of ministry *or* succession of teaching, but *both* succession of ministry *and* succession of teaching, bearing fruit in apostolic mission. If we take the either/or approach, we will end up with both a defect of ministry and a defect of teaching. Let us not weaken each other, but strengthen the church by giving it both the fullness of the catholic ministry and the soundness of catholic teaching.

III

For quite some time, the Anglican Communion has been in the forefront of ecumenical relations. Beginning with the Chicago Quadrilateral, adopted by the House of Bishops in 1886, The Episcopal Church has vigorously sought the reunion of Christendom.

However, the avowed policy of the Anglican Communion has been to insist upon theological agreement on matters of faith and order as a prerequisite to any form of intercommunion. This view is focused in Resolution 42 of the 1930 Lambeth Conference, which held "as a general principle that the intercommunion should be the goal of, rather than a means to, the restoration of union." This was reaffirmed in the declaration of the 1968 Lambeth Conference: "Reciprocal intercommunion (is) allowable . . . (only) where there is agreement on apostolic faith and order."

In September of 1982, the General Convention of The Episcopal Church passed Resolution A-37, calling for "Interim Eucharistic Sharing" with the Lutherans. There is not, as yet, agreement on the validity of Eucharist and ministry. Does Resolution A-37 create a state of intercommunion, and does it therefore violate the Anglican principle of intercommunion as the goal of, rather than a means to, Christian unity? And does that Resolution provide for a kind of concelebration of the Eucharist that might imply a mutual recognition of Orders?

In view of these questions, and the claim of the secular press that we have, in fact, established intercommunion with the Lutherans, it is of extreme importance that we examine the Resolution, and see clearly what the Church has actually done.

First, we have not approved either intercommunion, nor concelebration in the strict sense, both of which imply recognition of Orders. The original Resolution would have

This article originally appeared in *The Living Church* in January, 1983. Used by permission.

done both. However, the Resolution was rewritten prior to Convention, and the Lutheran Churches agreed to the changes.

As to intercommunion, the Resolution, A-37, declares that the Churches authorize further dialogue to discuss "outstanding questions that must be resolved before full communion (*communio in sacris*/altar and pulpit fellowship) can be established between the respective churches, e.g., implications of the Gospel, historic episcopate, and ordering of ministry (bishops, priests and deacons) in the total context of apostolicity." In the Explication attached to the Resolution we read: "Because final recognition of each other's eucharists or ministries has not yet been achieved, however, the proposed text does not constitute what otherwise might be called 'reciprocal intercommunion'."

The Joint Statement made by the three Lutheran Presiding Bishops and our own Primate contains the following language: "It (the Resolution) does not signify that 'final recognition' of each other's eucharists and ministries has yet been achieved. . . . This is not to be understood as 'reciprocal intercommunion' but rather a new and unique interim relationship which looks toward future steps in that direction."

This is in complete accord with the previous statements of the Lambeth Conference.

What the Resolution does is to state that we find the *teaching* of the Lutheran Churches to be sufficiently correct in regard to the Eucharist to justify allowing Lutherans to receive at our altars under the guidelines adopted by General Convention in 1979: "The Episcopal Church extends a special welcome to members of these three Lutheran Churches to receive Holy Communion in it under the Standard for Occasional Eucharist Sharing of its 1979 Convention." This is because the Lutheran Churches possess "Eucharistic teaching sufficient for Interim Sharing of the Eucharist."

While the Lutheran Churches also have extended an invitation to Anglicans to likewise receive at their altars, the invitation is not accepted by the Episcopal Church for its members. Indeed, as the Explication states: "Neither Episcopalians nor Lutherans *as Churches* declare here that they reciprocally *accept* on behalf of their members this invitation." Instead, "individual members of each Church are left to make their own decisions about whether to accept the invitation from the other."

As a matter of fact, many Lutherans might have some conscientious objection to receiving at altars presided over by priests whose theology might be highly questionable. Likewise, Anglicans would certainly object to receiving at altars where the president of the Eucharist might be a lay person (a practice permitted in many Lutheran Churches), and might find it impossible to receive from a minister who is not in the Apostolic Succession. Hence, it would not have been proper for either Church to accept, as an official action, an invitation to receive communion in the other Church.

Thus we can see that there is absolutely no state of intercommunion. We have said that Lutherans possess sufficient teaching of Sacrifice and Real Presence to meet the standards adopted in 1979 to receive communion in the Episcopal Church, and we invite them to do so. While they extend the same invitation to us, we do not formally accept the invitation, leaving the matter up to individual conscience, for good reason. Further, both in the document and the formal Joint Statement, great pains have been taken to make it perfectly clear that this is *not* intercommunion, that there cannot be intercommunion until there is a final agreement on the questions of the historic episcopate and the threefold ministry of Apostolic Succession. Indeed, the Resolution states clearly that it is not intended to imply any recognition by one church of the validity of either the Eucharist or ministry of another church.

As to the matter of concelebration, the term "concelebration" was deliberately not used in the Resolution, as it might imply the recognition that we do not yet have. The word concelebration is not part of our traditional theological vocabulary, and in recent years it has been used with a variety of implications. Instead, a new term was adopted, "common, joint celebration." As to this common joint celebration, the Resolution states:

> "The presence of an ordained minister of each participating Church at the altar in this way reflects the presence of two or more Churches expressing unity in faith and baptism *as well as* the remaining divisions which they seek to overcome; *however,* this does not imply . . . final recognition of either Church's Eucharist or ministry." (Emphasis added.)

The Explication more succinctly states:

"Clearly, then, neither Church's ministry is here... finally recognized. Final recognition itself could only follow upon resolution of the subjects proposed for further discussion (e.g. historic episcopate). Nonetheless, it may be said, if the proposed resolution is approved, that the Episcopal Church and these Lutheran Churches are now within these limits willing for their ordained clergy symbolically to stand together at the altar, although not yet *in place of each other* there."

The Joint Statement of the Presiding Bishops said the same thing in almost the same words: "The presence of an ordained minister of each participating Church at the altar is a sign of both 'unity of faith and baptism' as well as 'the remaining divisions which they seek to overcome.' These churches are now willing for their ordained clergy symbolically to stand together at the altar, although not yet in place of each other there."

The rules for a common, joint celebration are spelled out in Resolution A-44 of General Convention, which made six requirements: 1. "a priest or bishop of this Church shall be the celebrant or one of the celebrants"; 2. "the elements used are those used by our Lord Himself, namely bread and wine"; 3. "our Lord's Words of Institution be used"; 4. "the said priest or bishop join in the consecration of the gifts in a joint celebration"; 5. "any of the blessed elements remaining at the end of the service be reverently consumed"; 6. "the service be authorized by the diocesan bishop."

These guidelines are to be used, not only for common, joint celebration with the Lutheran Churches, but also for other occasions, such as those involving the Consultation On Church Union (as previously allowed). In other words, a common, joint celebration does not in any way imply mutual recognition of Orders. If we have a mutual recognition of Orders, then the minister of either Church may stand in the place of the other at the altar, as for example, is true with the European Old Catholics, the Philippine Independent Catholic Church, or the Mar Thoma Church of India. This is not presently permitted, either with Lutherans or the COCU Churches.

In conclusion, what the Episcopal Church has done does not provide either for intercommunion or for concelebration in the strict sense. It does not violate the guidelines previously proclaimed. It does not recognize Lutheran Orders. But it does allow for a closer cooperation with Lutherans, and recognizes a great similarity in theological understanding of sacraments and faith. As such, this is a significant and potentially constructive step. For this reason, we applaud the careful and thoughtful negotiation that has gone into it. It calls for new dialogue to begin in 1983, to deal with those questions which still separate us, such as the historic episcopate, and calls for a resolution of these issues before we can enter into a real and mutually longed-for, intercommunion.

BIBLIOGRAPHY

Authorized Version of the Holy Bible. Cambridge: Cambrige University Press, 1971.
Barber, John, *Patmos and the Seven Churches of Asia.* Bridgeport, 1851.
Barclay, William, *Introducing the Bible.* Nashville: Abingdon Press, 1972.
Bible Encyclopedia, 3 Vol., Howard-Severance Co., 1907.
Bicknell, E. J., *A Theological Introduction to the Thirty Nine Articles of the Church of England.* Longmans, 1959.
Bilson, Thomas, *Perpetual Government of Christ's Church.* Oxford: Oxford University Press, 1842.
The Book of Common Prayer. Church Pension Fund. 1945.
Canon Law of the Church of England, a Report of the Archbishops' Commission on Canon Law. London: SPCK, 1947.
Carter, Thomas, *The Doctrine of the Priesthood in the Church of England.* London: J. Masters and Co., 1876.
Catechismus ex decrete Concilii Tridentini. Rome: Sacred Congregation for the Propagation of the Faith, 1891.
Catholicity. a Report to the Archbishop of Canterbury, Westminister: Dacre Press, 1952.
Chapin, A. B., *The Primitive Church.* New Haven: Yale University Press, 1880.
Clarke, W. K. Lowther (Ed.), *Liturgy and Worship.* London: SPCK, 1964.
Concordance to the American Book of Common Prayer, Church Hymnal Corporation, 1970.
Constitution and Canons for the Government of the Protestant Episcopal Church in the United States of America, Otherwise known as the Episcopal Church, 1979.
Crane, Frank (Ed.), *The Lost Books of the Bible and the Forgotten Books of Eden.* New York: New American Library, 1974.
Cross, F. L. and Livingstone, E. A. (Ed.), *The Oxford Dictionary of the Christian Church.* Oxford: Oxford University Press, 1977.
Cruden, Alexander, *Cruden's Complete Concordance,* John C. Winston Company, 1949.
Dawley, Powel Mills, Volume II, Church's Teaching Series, *Chapters in Church History.* New York: Seabury Press, 1953.
Dentan, Robert C., Volume I, Church's Teaching Series, *The Holy Scriptures.* New York: Seabury Press, 1953.
Dispensation in Practice and Theory, The Report of the Archbishop of Canterbury's Commission. London: SPCK, 1944.
Dix, Dom Gregory, *Power of God,* Morehouse-Gorham Co., 1953; *The Question of Anglican Orders.* Westminister: Dacre Press, 1956; *Shape of the Liturgy.* Westminister: Dacre Press, 1954.
Doctrine in the Church of England, The Report of the Commission on Christian Doctrine appointed by the Archbishops of Canterbury and York in 1922, London: SPCK, 1950.
Echlin, E. P., SJ, *The Anglican Eucharist in Ecumenical Perspective.* New York: Seabury Press, 1968.
Ecumenical Bulletin, No. 33, January-February 1979, Seabury Service Center.
Ecumenical Bulletin, No. 38, November-December 1979, Seabury Service Center.
Ehrhardt, A., *The Apostolic Succession.* London: Lutterworth Press, 1953.
The Episcopal Church Annual of 1953. New York: Morehouse-Gorham Co., 1952.
The Episcopal Church Annual of 1962. New York: Morehouse-Barlow Co., 1961.

The Episcopal Church Annual of 1971. New York: Morehouse-Barlow Co., 1970

Fairweather, E. R., *Episcopacy Re-Asserted.* London: A. R. Mowbray and Co., 1955.

Gams, Pius Bonifacius, OSB, *Series Episcoporum Ecclesiae Catholicae.* Leipzig: K. W. Hiersemann, 1931.

Gore, Charles (Ed.), *A New Commentary on Holy Scripture.* New York: The Macmillan Company, 1958.

Hadden, A. W., *Apostolical Succession.* London: Rivingtons, 1879.

Hall, Francis J., Dogmatic Theology, Volume II, *Authority;* Volume IV, *The Trinity;* Volume VI, *The Incarnation;* Volume VIII, *The Church and the Sacramental System;* Volume IX, *The Sacraments:* American Church Union, 1969.

Haselmeyer, L. A., *Lambeth and Unity.* New York: Morehouse-Gorham Co., 1948.

The History of the Christian Church, Vol. I. Milwaukee: The Young Churchman Co., 1913.

Holy Baptism and a Form for Confirmation, Church Hymnal Corporation, 1975.

Hooker, Richard, *Ecclesiastical Polity.* New York: The Macmillan Company, 1902.

Hughes, John Jay, *Stewards of the Lord.* London: Sheed & Ward, 1970.

Hughes, Phillip E., *Theology of the English Reformers.* London: Hodder and Stoughton, 1965.

Hughson, S. C., *The Seven Sacraments,* Holy Cross Press, 1950.

Jenkins, Claude, and Mackenzie, K.D., (Ed.), *Episcopacy Ancient and Modern.* London: SPCK, 1930.

Jones, Cheslyn: Wainwright, Geoffrey; and Yarnold, Edward, S. J., (Ed.), *The Study of Liturgy.* Oxford: Oxford University Press, 1978.

Journal of the General Convention of the Protestant Episcopal Church in the U.S.A., 1961.

Journal of the General Convention of the Protestant Episcopal Church in the U.S.A., 1979.

Kelly, J. N. D., *Early Christian Doctrines.* New York: Harper & Row, 1960.

Lace, O. Jessie (Ed.), *Understanding the New Testament.* Cambridge: Cambridge University Press, 1965.

Lambeth Conference 1968 Resolutions and Reports, SPCK and Seabury Press, 1968.

Lane, C. A., *Illustrated Notes on English Church History,* 2 Vol. London: SPCK, 1899.

Lawson, John, *A Theological and Historical Introduction to the Apostolic Fathers.* New York: The Macmillan Co., 1961.

Mason, A. J., *The Church of England and Episcopacy.* Cambridge: Cambridge University Press, 1914.

Mason, Francis, *Vindication of the Church of England,* London, 1728.

Mellor, Enid B. (Ed.), *The Making of the Old Testament.* Cambridge: Cambridge University Press, 1972

Montizembert, Eric, *This We Believe.* New York: Morehouse-Barlow Co., 1951.

Moorman, J. R. H., *A History of the Church in England.* New York: Morehouse-Barlow Co., 1954.

Moss, C. B., *The Christian Faith.* New York: Morehouse-Gorham Co., 1957.

Neill, Stephen, *Anglicanism.* London: Penguin Publishers, 1958.

The New English Bible with the Apocrypha. Oxford: Oxford University Press, 1970.

Overall, John, *Convocation Book.* Oxford: Oxford University Press, 1844.

Perceval, A. P., *The Doctrine of Apostolic Succession.* New York: P. E. Tract Society, 1839.

BIBLIOGRAPHY

Phillimore, Sir Walter George Frank, *The Esslesiastical Law of the Church of England*, 2 Vol., 2nd Ed. London: Sweet and Maxwell, 1895.
Pike, James A. and Pittinger, W. Norman, Volume III, Church's Teaching Series, *The Faith of the Church*. New York: Seabury Press, 1952.
Prayer Book Studies IV, *The Eucharistic Liturgy*, Church Pension Fund, 1953.
Prayer Book Studies 26, *Holy Baptism together with a Form for Confirmation*, Church Hymnal Corporation, 1973.
Procter, Francis, and Frere, Walter H., *A New History of the Book of Common Prayer*. New York: Macmillan and Co., 1951.
Proposed Book of Common Prayer. New York: Seabury Press, 1977.
Reed, J. S., *The Bishop's Blue Book*. New York: James Pott and Co., 1874.
Riley, Hugh M., *Christian Initiation*, Catholic University Press, 1974.
St. Augustine of Hippo, *An Augustine Synthesis*, edited by Erich Przywara. New York: Harper & Brothers, 1958.
St. Thomas Aquinas, *Summa Theologica*, Introduction edited by Anton C. Pegis. New York: Random House, 1948.
Seabury, W. J., *Lectures on Haddan's Apostolical Succession*. New York: Crothers and Korth, 1893.
Selwyn, Edward Gordon (Ed.), *Essays Catholic & Critical*. London: SPCK, 1958.
Shepherd, Massey H., Jr., Volume IV, Church's Teaching Series, *The Worship of the Church*, Seabury Press, 1953; *The Oxford American Prayer Book Commentary*. Oxford: Oxford University Press, 1973.
Spivey, Robert A. and Smith, D. Moody, Jr., *Anatomy of the New Testament*. New York: Macmillan Publishing Co., 1974.
Stevick, Daniel B., *Supplement to Prayer Book Studies 26*, Church Hymnal Corp., 1973.
Stubbs, William, *Registrum Sacrum Anglicanum*. Oxford: Oxford University Press, 1858.
Waterman, Lucius, *Tables of Episcopal Descent*. New York: Edwin Gorham, 1903.
Whatley, Richard, *Apostolic Succession Considered*. London: Longmans, Green and Co., 1912.
Witsell, W. P., *Our Church One Through the Ages*. New York: Edwin Gorham, 1923.